IMAGES OF WAR

PARTISANS & GUERRILLAS OF WORLD WAR TWO

Dedicated to My Family

IMAGES OF WAR

PARTISANS & GUERRILLAS OF WORLD WAR TWO

POLAND, THE SOVIET UNION, CZECHOSLOVAKIA, ITALY, FRANCE

PHILIP JOWETT

Pen & Sword

MILITARY

AN IMPRINT OF PEN & SWORD BOOKS LTD.
YORKSHIRE ~ PHILADELPHIA

First published in Great Britain in 2026 by
Pen & Sword Military
An imprint of
Pen & Sword Books Ltd
Yorkshire – Philadelphia

ISBN 978 1 39903 797 6

Typeset in 12/14 Gill Sans by
Typeset by SJmagic DESIGN SERVICES, India.
Printed and bound in England by CPI Group (UK) Ltd., Croydon.

The Publisher's authorised representative in the EU for product safety is Authorised Rep Compliance Ltd., Ground Floor, 71 Lower Baggot Street, Dublin D02 P593, Ireland.
www.arccompliance.com

For a complete list of Pen & Sword titles please contact

PEN & SWORD BOOKS LIMITED
George House, Units 12 & 13, Beevor Street, Off Pontefract Road,
Barnsley, South Yorkshire, S71 1HN, England
E-mail: enquiries@pen-and-sword.co.uk
Website: www.pen-and-sword.co.uk

or

PEN AND SWORD BOOKS
1950 Lawrence Rd, Havertown, PA 19083, USA
E-mail: uspen-and-sword@casematepublishers.com
Website: www.penandswordbooks.com

Contents

Prelude.. 6

Introduction.. 7

Chapter One
Poland 1939-1945 9

Chapter Two
Soviet Partisans 1941-1944 31

Chapter Three
German Partisan Operations 1941-1944 56

Chapter Four
Soviet Partisan Warfare 1943-1944......................... 78

Chapter Five
Axis Anti-Partisan Forces in Russia 1941-1944..... 101

Chapter Six
The Warsaw Risings 1943-1944.............................. 125

Chapter Seven
Czechoslovakia 1940-1944 147

Chapter Eight
Italian Partisans 171

Chapter Nine
Italian Partisans & Fascists.................................... 194

Chapter Ten
French Resistance 1940-1944 216

Prelude

Partisan and guerrilla warfare in Europe during The Second World War was present in all the countries occupied by the German, Italian and other Axis forces. This first volume on the history of these irregular forces covers Poland, the Soviet Union, Italy and France from 1939 until 1945. A second book will feature the many and diverse partisan forces in the Balkans including Greece, Yugoslavia and Albania. The partisans and guerrillas were themselves often made up of diverse groups with many having Communist sympathies. Other groups were anti-Communist and fought with the partisans who were under the command of left-wing leaders like Tito in Yugoslavia and Enver Hoxha in Albania. Soviet partisans were nearly all Communists and were more united than the groups from other countries. There were, however, partisan groups in the Baltic and the Ukraine who resisted the Communists as well as the German Army. In Italy, Greece, Albania and Yugoslavia the partisans and guerrillas openly fought each in a struggle for the future control of their countries. Yugoslavian guerrillas were divided into pro-Communist partisans and right wing-Chetniks who at times cooperated with the German occupiers.

Introduction

This book describes in words and images the anti-German and anti-Italian partisan and guerrilla forces of Europe during the 1939–1945 period. The aggressive war aims of Nazi Germany and Fascist Italy turned the 1930s into a period of constant encroachment on the weaker nations in Central Europe and the Balkans. From the late 1930s until 1941, the expansion of Hitler's Germany saw Czechoslovakia, Poland and the Scandinavian nations of Norway and Denmark come under Nazi control. With the fall of the Netherlands, Belgium and then France in 1940, Hitler was in control of most of Western Europe. Mussolini's Balkan adventures in 1939, with a walkover conquest of Albania and then failure in the invasion of Greece 1940, dragged Hitler into involvement in the Balkans. Greece and Yugoslavia were conquered in April 1941 and the latter was dismembered in a similar way that Czechoslovakia had been in 1938–39. With Hitler ready to launch his anti-Bolshevik 'crusade' with his invasion of Soviet Russia in June 1941, the map of pre-1939 Europe had been totally redrawn.

None of the peoples of these conquered nations were prepared to accept the brutal rule of both Germany and Italy and they began to organise armed resistance. This book is the first of two volumes to describe, in a collection of photographs and text, the partisans and guerrillas who fought their countries' occupation. Some countries have not been included as I have decided only to include resistance forces who raised mass units during the 1939 – 45 period. This does not in any way disregard the 'contribution' of the resistance forces in Belgium, the Netherlands, Luxembourg and the Scandinavian nations who fought courageously against German occupation. They all performed vital intelligence work on behalf of the Allies and undermined the German occupation. Resistance to the Axis occupation took two forms: open, overt or guerrilla war, and underground or covert resistance. Resistance forces in Belgium (Belgisch verzet,) the Netherlands (Nederland verzet) and Denmark (Den Danske modstandsbevegelse) fought German occupation using covert tactics. The topography and the density of the population in these three countries did not allow for overt guerrilla resistance. Norway's forests and mountains did allow for some overt resistance by the Milorg resistance forces. Most of their actions against the Germans were, however, by small sabotage units which suffered 1,433 killed during the war including 255 women. Towards the end of the conflict 8,000 Norwegians were given secret training in neutral Sweden. These forces were then available to aid the Allied liberation of Norway when they crossed the border and then came out into the open to disarm German and collaborationist forces.

When the German Armies conquered Eastern Europe and the Balkans from 1939 until 1945 they faced resistance from armed groups from these countries. These partisans were to prove a thorn in the side of the occupying forces, with guerrilla attacks against the Germans. Other Axis forces, including Italy pre-1943, Hungary and Slovakia, also faced resistance from the regions they occupied alongside the German army. The partisans were usually full-time fighters who lived in the forest and mountain encampments and struck at the occupiers with ferocity. They blew up trains, attacked local garrisons and assassinated anyone who had collaborated with the occupying forces. Savage reprisals against the partisans and the general civilian population only caused more bitterness and further resistance from the anti-Axis guerrillas.

Chapter One

Poland 1939-1945

Out of all the European nations involved in the Second World War, Poland was to suffer the worst, beginning in September 1939. Poles were seen by the German occupiers as racially inferior, while the Soviets were almost as brutal in Eastern Poland which they ruled until the German invasion of the Soviet Union in June 1941. One commentator said that the fate of Poland between 1939 and 1945 was frightful, 'almost beyond comprehension'. The brutal German Governor of Poland, Hans Frank, was quoted as saying that the Polish people's fate was that 'mincemeat could be made of them'. Any sign of resistance by the Poles would be dealt with by extreme brutality which temporarily tempered the Polish people's wish to fight their occupiers. It soon became apparent, however, that life under German rule would be so unbearable that many thought that they had nothing to lose by resisting. The horrific treatment by the Nazis of the large Jewish population, which made up 10 per cent of the total Polish population, was of course even worse that the treatment meted out to the Poles. It ended with the mass extermination of the majority of the 3.5 million Jewish people, with only 380,000 surviving the war. Any Jews who escaped captivity and fled into the countryside tried to take shelter with the sometimes hostile Polish resistance.

Regardless of the dire consequences for any defiance, the first plans for resistance to the German and Russian occupiers were made as early as September 1939. In late 1939 the resistance was known as the Sluzba Zwyciestwu Polski – SZP – 'Service for Poland's Victory' but from mid-November it became the 'Union of Armed Struggle' – ZWZ, with a strength of 40,000 fighters by September 1940. In the interim between the fall of Poland in September 1939 and the defeat of France in June 1940 the Polish government-in-exile was based in Paris. On 14 February 1942 the ZWZ changed its name to the Home Army – Armia Krajowa, by which it was known until 1945. In 1942 the AK had 100,000 fighters. By spring 1944, the AK had 8,920 platoons with a total estimated strength of 380–400,000 fighters. The AK was loyal to the Polish government-in-exile in London and received its orders from General Sikorski, the head of the government. The AK was in fact an umbrella organisation made up of 200 political organisations and military units. Some AK units were full time partisans supported by the bulk of the Polish population and many continued to wear their 1939 uniforms. Arms were at first taken from the Polish Army stores or from arms stashes hastily buried in September 1939. Many small arms were found to have deteriorated when the Home Army dug them up and armaments remained a major problem for them. Because of the shortage of arms and supplies some fighters lived among the population, only operating when the AK needed reinforcements. From 1940 onwards the Home Army began to attack the trains taking supplies to the German garrisons in Western Poland. From June 1941 the situation in Poland changed drastically when Germany launched 'Operation Barbarossa' – the invasion of the Soviet Union. Poland became the main transit route for the German Army's vast amount of supplies heading for the Eastern Front. Attacks against the German infrastructure increased drastically in the second half of 1941. During this period they managed to destroy 1,935 train engines and derailed ninety trains while also blowing up three bridges and setting on fire 257 lorries.

With the German breaking of the Non-Aggression Pact of 1939, the Soviet Union now decided to set up their own pro-Soviet resistance group which they named the 'Union of Polish Patriots' in Russia. Polish Communists were parachuted into Poland in 1942 where they set up an underground 'Workers Party'. Their next step of course was to begin to organise their own partisan units, which they called 'Peoples Guards'. Any hope of a meaningful alliance between the AK and the PG was ended when thousands of Polish army officers' bodies were discovered in the woods around Katyn in April 1943. It soon became obvious that these men had been taken captive during the Russian invasion of Eastern Poland in 1939 and were later taken to the woods and shot. The AK leadership saw this slaughter as a sign of things to come if the Soviet Union ever came back into Poland. For the rest of the war and into the late 1940s the rivalry and hatred between the pro- and anti-Communist Polish armed group was to continue. Other partisan groups which operated in Poland included the Narodowa Organizacja Wojskowa (NOW), which was formed from supporters of the National Party in October 1939 and was absorbed by the AK in 1942. Another group which remained aloof of the AK were the 'Peasant Battalions' raised from members of the pre-1939 Peasants' Party in August 1940.

From 1942 until early 1944 the AK launched a series of major operations against the German occupiers. 'Operation Garland' in 1942 and 'Operation Jula' in 1944 were aimed at sabotaging the German rail system. The 'Zamosc Rising' of 1943–44 was able to partly frustrate the mass deportation of Polish men to work as slave labourers in Germany. Their farms were to be taken over by German farmers who were to defend themselves with weapons and training provided by the Nazis. 'Operation Belt' of 1943 was another attempt to disrupt the occupation, this time with border outposts particularly targeted. A list of AK achievements during the 1941–44 period was quite impressive and indicated the problems that Polish resistance caused. The list includes 6,930 damaged locomotives, thirty-eight blown up bridges, 4,326 damaged motor vehicles, 25,145 acts of sabotage and 5,733 assassinations of German military and civilians. Unlike in other occupied countries in the Second World War there were few collaborators for the AK to deal with as the Poles were not deemed to be worth employing by the Germans. One notable success for the assassination squads was the killing of SS-General Franz Kutschera, who was shot outside the SS HQ in Warsaw. Another extremely important role for Polish resisters was the supplying of intelligence by them to the government-in-exile and the British intelligence services in London. British intelligence reported that the vast amount of information supplied by the Poles was 'high quality' and was due to the skills of the 1,600 agents operating in Poland.

1943 was also the year that the AK suffered two major blows when its leader in Poland General Grot-Rowecki was arrested in a widespread crackdown on their leadership by the Germans. A few days later the Polish military leader in exile, General Sikorski, was shot down in a plane over Gibraltar. Both men were soon replaced but not by officers of the same calibre, with the AK commander now being General Bor-Komorowski, and in London by General Sosnkowski. Despite these setbacks the AK still continued to launch its attacks against the German occupiers throughout 1943 and into 1944, who were now being pushed back on the Eastern Front. In early 1944 the AK launched its long-planned Operation 'Burza' or 'Tempest', which was really an intensified version of what they had been doing for several years. There was disputes over the targets for 'Tempest', with some arguing that the main attacks should be in the countryside while others wanted to strike in the cities. In the end it was decided that the main objective for the operation would be an uprising in the capital, Warsaw. This operation was planned to coincide with the arrival of the Soviet Red Army in the suburbs of the city which was expected during July 1944.

(**Above**) A unit of the Home Army forms in a Polish village without uniforms but with plenty of rifles left over from the 1939 invasion. The Polish people were too proud to give up the struggle after the German and Russian invasions of their homeland. Instead they formed units of fighters, often from the many Polish Army formations that had been left behind in the aftermath of the Blitzkrieg of September 1939. (*Author's Collection*)

(**Opposite, above**) Major Henryk Dobrzanski, who was known by his nickname 'Major Hubal', was the leader of the first partisan unit in the Second World War. He was in his early 40s in 1939 when he served as second in command to a reserve Polish cavalry regiment. His military career had involved service during the First World War and then in the 1920 war with the Russian Red Army. When the Polish Army surrendered in late September 1939, 'Hubal' and 180 of his men refused to give up the fight and rode into the countryside. Hubal's force was soon reduced to a hard core of fifty men who tried to break out of Poland in an attempt to get to join the Poles forming an émigré army in France. When this proved impossible, the so-called 'Detached Unit of the Polish Army' spent the late autumn and winter attacking German units before riding back into the forests. By spring 1940 the unit was running out of luck, and on 30 April Hubal and another officer were killed in a German ambush. The brave commander's body was put on public display by the Germans like a hunting trophy. Some of his men continued to fight until 25 June, when the remains of the unit disbanded and tried to make their individual way out of Poland. (*Author's Collection, Public Domain*)

(**Below**) These men of Major Hubal's command stand with their commander Jozef Walicki (fourth from right), and pose in the snow of the winter of 1939–40. The partisan group organised by Major Hubal was known as the 'Detached Unit of the Polish Army'. Hubal had been assigned to the 110th Reserve Cavalry Regiment shortly before the outbreak of war. Most of his men did not get the chance to receive their basic training pre-September 1939 and had to learn the art of guerrilla war as they fought. (*Author's Collection*)

(**Above**) Men of the AK Wilenskiej Brigade take part in their unit roll call wearing their winter uniforms and most have fur-collared jackets. Units like this operated in the Polish countryside with the support of the local population but the price paid by the civilians was high. In reality, lightly armed units like this could not defend positions for long against the Luftwaffe's bombers and German armoured forces. (*Private Collection*)

(**Opposite, above**) A Polish Home Army radio post operates in early 1944 in the build up to the Warsaw Rising in August. From the end of 1939 the Poles had begun organised resistance to the brutal German occupation. By 1944 the Armia Krajowa had a strength of 400,000 fighters and supporters in the field but only a fraction were properly armed. As with every other military item needed to run a resistance force, radios would have been taken from hidden caches left over from September 1939 or air dropped by the Allies. (*Author's Collection, Public Domain*)

(**Opposite, below**) Members of a AK unit do their best to patch up a wounded comrade in their forest base in the early days of the resistance against the Germans. The medical and other resources available to AK units varied greatly with the larger groups usually having more trained personnel. Any Polish doctor who dared assist their local AK unit was of course executed by the Germans if they were revealed to be aiding the 'bandits'. (*Author's Collection, Public Domain*)

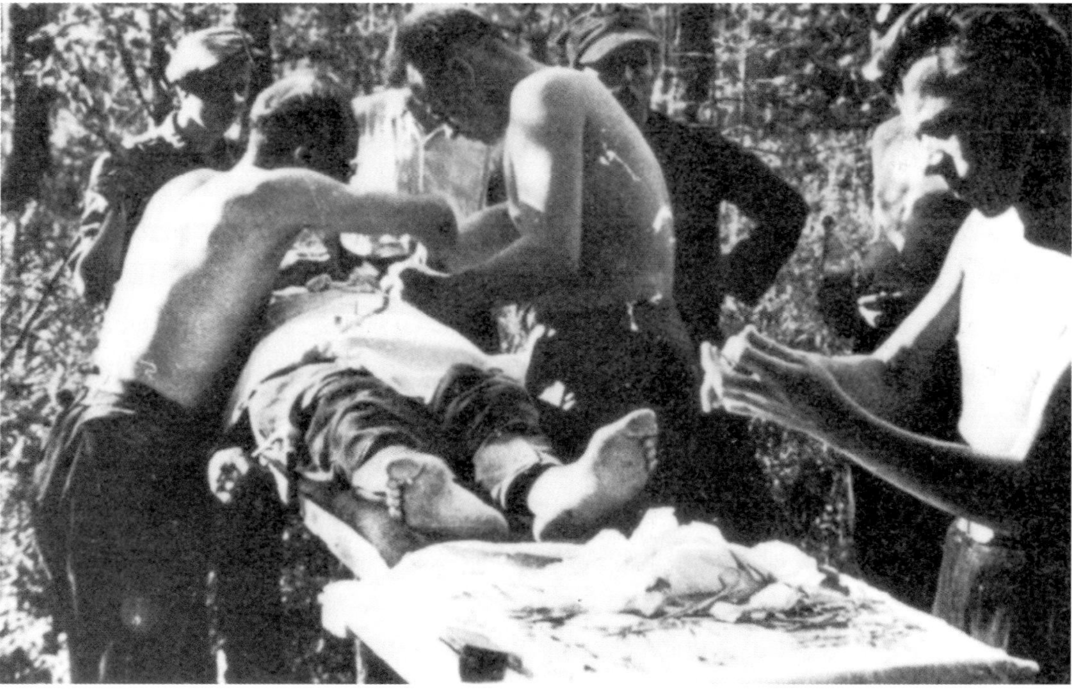

Armia Krajowa fighters of the 5th Company of the 25th Home Army infantry fire from cover during a training exercise. Two men are armed with the standard Polish rifle, the Karabinek Mauser 7.92mm wz.98 and an Austrian MG-30 which was also used by the German Army. (*Author's Collection, Public Domain*)

Two child partisans pose in their forest base proudly showing off their rifle and carbine to their comrades. The two boys, Orlicz and Tomek, were not surprisingly the two youngest fighters in this Armia Krajowa unit. Orlicz is armed with a French Lebel carbine which is probably a left over from the 1920 war against the Soviet Union. (*Author's Collection, Public Domain*)

This group of Armia Krajowa fighters belong to the 'Watra IV' unit and are well armed with rifles, carbines and hand grenades. Their nicknames are from left to right, 'Dab', 'Lis', 'Jelen', 'Zagloba', 'Wilk', 'NN' and 'Rys'. (*Author's Collection, Public Domain*)

This AK fighter belongs to the 1st Company of the 'Stalowy' and 'Dziobak' forest units which operated around the city of Drohobych. The city had been part of the 2nd Polish Republic until September 1939 when it was ceded to the Soviet Union as part of the Ukrainian Socialist Republic. He is armed with a German submachine gun, one of the types that predated the MP-40 in common used during 1939–45. (*Author's Collection, Public Domain*)

A Polish fighter fires from cover with his 7.92mm *reczny karabin maszynowy* Browning Wz 30 automatic-rifle. The Polish Army in 1939 used this licence-produced version of the US Browning and a few of this weapon ended up in Armia Krajowa hands. (*Author's Collection, Public Domain*)

These three AK fighters belong to the Company of Lieutenant Jerzy Sztagirwalk, who was known as 'Rozlog'. This unit was part of the 72nd Infantry Regiment of the Armia Krajowa which operated along the Pilica River in Central Poland. Two of the men are armed with Polish Mausers while the man in the centre of the trio, Corporal Marian Gawdzik, proudly shows off his German MG-42 with spare ammunition draped over his shoulders. (*Private Collection, Public Domain*)

Ulhan Kazimierz Nowicki from the AK 'Kampinos Group' poses in full Polish pre-1939 uniform with a captured MP-40 submachine gun. The Kampinos Group fought in the Kampinos Forest during the Warsaw Rising and then during Operation Tempest. It fought a total of forty-seven battles and skirmishes and cleared the central and eastern parts of the forest. Fighters from the Kampinos Group attacked German targets in the suburbs of Warsaw in support of the rising in August 1944. (*Private Collection, Public Domain*)

A Cavalry Squadron of the 3rd AK Guerrilla Brigade leave their base in the town of Turgiele close to Vilnius to go on patrol. Mounted units could only survive in the more remote regions of Poland as the Luftwaffe would find these troops an easy target if caught in the open. The young rider at the back of the column looks back at the camera and appears to be a female member of the squadron. (*Private Collection, Public Domain*)

AK Fighters of the 77th Home Army Infantry Regiment smile for the camera in January 1944. Most of the group are well dressed for the Polish winter with greatcoats and fur lined coats as well as woollen scarves. Of course surviving in the winter was difficult for the Home Army, especially if local support was withdrawn due to the brutal tactics of the Germans. (*Author's Collection*)

Lieutenant Jan Piwinik known as 'Ponury' – the commander of the 7th Battalion of the 77th AK Infantry Regiment accepts the oath from the newly raised 2nd Company. This photograph was taken in May 1944 in the Nowogródek Region which is now part of Belarus. To the right of the oath table is a Soviet Maxim M1910 heavy machine gun, probably captured during the 1920–21 war between the Russians and Poland. (*NAC*)

A Home Army fighter stands guard in front of a church door while his officers discuss an operation in 1943. He is well dressed for winter fighting with an army tunic worn under a wool-lined coat and has a *rogatywka* field cap. His cavalry boots suggest that he belongs to a cavalry unit, with most AK groups including a mounted section at least. (*NAC*)

(**Opposite, above**) Soldiers of the 27th Division of the Armia Krajowa take a rest during operations in the Volhynia region in the summer of 1944. Formed in January 1944 the 6,500 strong 27th was raised to try and protect the Polish minority from Ukrainian Nationalists in Volhynia and Eastern Galicia. Volhynia was the scene of a number of massacres of the Polish minority by Ukrainians in 1943. The longstanding hostility between the Ukrainians and the Poles, who they saw as a threat, resulted in the deaths of up to 100,000 men, women and children. By March 1943 the 27th had grown to 7,300 fighters and was soon fighting alongside local Polish volunteers against the Ukrainian Insurgent Army – UPA (*Author's Collection – Public Domain*)

(**Opposite, below**) Armia Krajowa fighters are seen training with a Soviet DP-28 light machine gun that their unit has acquired. The Degtyaryov-made machine gun was the standard weapon of the Red Army during the whole of the Second World War. These weapons were supplied to the Soviet raised 1st Polish Army and may have found their way in small numbers from sympathetic soldiers of the pro-Communist force. (*Private Collection – Public Domain*)

(**Above**) Polish fighters gather together to show off the wide variety of weapons they have to defend themselves with. They belong to the AK 51st Infantry Regiment which was based in the Drohobych region. Arms carried by the men include several PPSH-41 submachine guns and a number of Sten Mk IIs which had been air dropped into their forest positions. (*Private Collection – Public Domain*)

(**Opposite, above**) An AK unit rests in the forest and examine their weapons, including two PPSH-41 Soviet submachine guns and a few Polish Mausers. They are fighting in and around the Sambor Forest and their names are from left to right: Jozef Loreth (known as 'Warsawawiak'), 'Emanuel', Unknown, Sergeant Stan Slaw Mazurkiewicz (known as 'Leos') and Zbigniew Loreth. (*Private Collection – Public Domain*)

(**Opposite, below**) These men belong to the 1st Company of the Sambor District Forest unit of the AK and apart from one of the men they are armed with Polish Mauser rifles. Sambor on the Polish-Ukrainian border had been part of Poland until 1941, and under German rule was part of Western Ukraine. It was the site of a ghetto which housed 10,000 Jews who were sent to extermination camps, with a few escaping into the forest where they joined the partisans. The last Jews in the ghetto were collected up and trucked into the forest where they were shot in June 1943. (*Private Collection – Public Domain*)

(**Above**) This AK unit, the 25th Infantry Regiment is armed mainly with Soviet rifles, submachine guns and a Maxim M1910 heavy machine gun. Although quantities of small arms did find their way into Home Army hands the relationship between the AK and the Soviet Union was not good. The Soviet Union considered the Home Army 'an impediment to the introduction of a Communist-friendly government in Poland post-war'. On the Polish side the discovery of almost 22,000 bodies of captured officers killed in the Katyn Forest by the NKVD in 1940 made the Soviet Union a deadly enemy. (*Private Collection – Public Domain*)

(**Opposite, above**) AK fighters take part in training close to their forest base near to the city of Drohobych in Western Ukraine, which had been part of Poland until 1941. These two men are not only fighting for the freedom of their city from the German occupiers, but in the Second World War were trying to keep their region in Poland. (*Private Collection – Public Domain*)

(**Opposite, below**) Fighters of the 'Osnowy' group of the AK 50th Infantry Regiment are part of a break through of the encirclement of the Pripyat in May 1944. Units like this had been under attack from the Ukrainian People's Army since 1943, when large numbers of Poles were killed in internecine fighting. (*Private Collection – Public Domain*)

This group of Polish fighters belong to the Peasant Battalions (Bataliony Chlopskie or BCh) which were created in mid-1940. Their men were followers of the Agrarian political, party or 'Peoples Party', who fought independently of the AK until 1944. Although not as well organised as the Armia Krajowa in the summer of 1944, the Peasant Battalions had up to 160,000 recruits many of whom were not armed. By 1944 some BCh units were integrated with the AK as political rivalries gave way to the need to unite against the shared enemy. (*Author's Collection*)

This young partisan is Stanislaw 'Szlomo' Szmajzner who was one of the fifty-eight survivors of Sobibor Extermination Camp in 1943. Sobibor, in German-occupied Poland, saw a mass breakout from the camp with most of the 600 men and boys who escaped being hunted down. Sixteen-year-old Szmajzner joined a group of about sixteen escapees who took to the forests but thirteen were killed by Polish Nationalists. This photograph taken shortly after his escape shows Szmajzner after joining a group of partisans and he is armed with a PPSH-41 submachine gun. (*Author's Collection*)

These well-armed Polish fighters all with MP-40s belong to the Armia Ludowa – 'AL' the Soviet raised People's Army, which was formed in early January 1944. This armed group was the successor to the Gwardia Ludowa, or People's Guard, and reached a strength of up to 30,000 men. Out of this total at least 5,000 were Russian volunteers who had been seconded into the AL. Reports said the Armia Ludowa had only 6,000 active fighters with the rest made up of support and second-line personnel. Once the AL had fulfilled its role it was disbanded on 29 July 1944 and most of its men were sent to the regular Polish Red Army – LWP. (*Author's Collection*)

Grzegorz Korczynski (1915–1971) was a Polish Communist commander of the pro-Moscow Gwardia Ludowa, having spent time in France working for the French Communist Party until 1942. He had fought on the Republican side during the Spanish Civil War until 1939 and then could not return safely to Poland. In August 1942 he was sent from France, where he had been in hiding, to Poland, where he secretly tried to organise partisans units in the Lublin region. He was a controversial character who was accused of war crimes against the Jews, while he was also reported to have saved Jews from captivity. Having fought from 1942 until 1944 with his partisan group he became commander of the Lublin District of the Polish People's Army, LWP. His role from 1945 to 1946 was the pacification of Polish villages who supported the Polish Home Army during their post-war battles against the pro-Soviet regime in Warsaw. (*Author's Collection*)

While the German occupiers were unwilling to recruit Polish men to work as anything other than slave labourers, the Poles were equally adamant that they would not collaborate with the occupiers. However, the Germans were willing to raise an auxiliary police force from among the German minority in Poland. This man is a volunteer for the Sonderdienst (Special Service) Auxiliary Police which recruited Germans between the ages of 18 and 40. The Governor of the General Government of Poland, Hans Frank, was hoping to turn this armed force into his own private force, loyal only to him. This was never going to be allowed as Himmler wanted to keep a tight control on any auxiliary forces in occupied Europe. (*NAC*)

Volunteers of the Sonderdienst – 'Special Service Auxiliary Police' march through the centre of Krakow in May 1940. These ethnic-Germans – *Volksdeutsche* were recruited in May 1940 but their ranks were later filled by Soviet prisoners of war. The Russians were often employed as Trawniki-manner – guards at the concentration camps around Poland. They were desperate men who were willing to obey German orders no matter how criminal and cruel in order to survive. (*NAC*)

Chapter Two

Soviet Partisans 1941-1944

When Nazi Germany launched the invasion of the Soviet Union 'Operation Barbarossa' in June 1941 there were no detailed plans for armed resistance to the invaders. Joseph Stalin, the Soviet leader, was still hoping that the non-aggression pact he had signed with Hitler on 23/24 August 1939 would hold. He did not want to anger the Nazi leader by organising a mass para-military force intended to defend Russia against an invading German Army. Of course as soon as Joseph Stalin and his leadership had recovered from the initial shock of the invasion they began planning armed resistance at all levels. On 18 July the Party Central Committee issued a directive for the organising of an underground partisan campaign. Stalin made a Radio Speech called for the setting up immediately of a partisan organisation and the Soviet leader called for:

> The setting up of partisan cavalry and infantry detachments and sabotage groups in enemy occupied areas for the struggle against units of the enemy army. To inflame partisan warfare everywhere and at all times to blow up bridges and roads, to spoil telephone communications, to set fire to forests, warehouses and wagons. To create unbearable conditions in the occupied areas for the enemy and all that him, to pursue and destroy them at every step to disrupt everything they do!

There was a ready-made force of up to 250,000 Russian soldiers caught behind the rapidly advancing German forces. Most of these men were armed but they were bewildered, confused and not really in a fit state to fight against the invaders. Their officers had little or no communication with Moscow and in the paranoid state that had existed in the Soviet Union, some were afraid to use their initiative. They were used to acting only on issued orders and feared for their lives if they formed armed groups without permission. Following Stalin's instructions on resistance, small armed groups did appear in all newly occupied regions of the Soviet Union. These groups faced the problem of the previously subdued hostility of much of the Russian population in the conquered territory towards Stalin. With Soviet authority removed overnight many Russians were shown to have little or no enthusiasm to fight for a much disliked state. Some early resistance was aggressive if expensive for the partisans with one unit with 123 rifles and two light machine guns going on a six-week spree. During this month and a half they launched twenty-five attacks, destroyed twenty lorries and killed 120 'Fascists', but at the end there were only twelve men left alive. Partisan morale fell sharply towards the end of 1941 as any initial enthusiasm was worn down by the reality of partisan warfare. Supplies were scarce, and during the winter of 1941 many partisans died from hunger and the cold, and any encounters with the occupying forces usually ended with heavy losses by the partisans. The wounded went untreated and partisan morale soon sank with no hope of any help coming from their political leaders. In many cases the local population who had endured several decades of mistreatment were not sympathetic to the partisan cause. It was left to the hardcore Communist Party members to keep the partisan movement alive and these included many veterans of the Civil War of 1917–22. It was also estimated that 70 per cent of the new partisan volunteers were card-carrying members of the Communist Youth Organisation. Although there were hundreds of partisan groups by 1942 they were often isolated and were not in contact with other nearby forces. The nature of the fighting meant that it was difficult making contact with other groups, especially in the early stages. During the winter of 1942–43 connections between groups did develop with groups in the Bryansk region, in the triangle between the Pripyat Marshes and the Dnieper river, and along the Orsha and Neva Rivers.

In Leningrad Province in north western Russia, 350 partisan Detachments of between thirty and fifty men were set up in the first months of the invasion. The first small groups had appeared in July–August 1941, and 191 were established in Leningrad itself to operate mostly in the west of the province. There were also thirty-six underground 'Party District Committees' established to help coordinate the partisan effort. All resistance groups in occupied Russia were to suffer heavy losses in the early days of their fight against the invader. In the first month of the invasion, 7,724 fighters were killed by the highly efficient Gestapo and the German Army. A total of forty-five detachments were totally wiped out along with an estimated twenty-four smaller partisan groups. In an attempt to make the partisan units more capable of fighting the invaders smaller groups were organised into brigades. In eastern Belorussia between July and September 1941 a total of 430 detachments were formed with 8,000 fighters being trained in 'partisan preparation centres'. From April 1942 special courses were run in unoccupied parts of Belorussia, with 3,000 cadets taking part and being formed into fifteen partisan detachments and 100 'organisational groups' and these were sent to penetrate the German rear areas. In July 1941 the Central Committee of the Belorussian Communist Party had sent the first groups behind German lines. They sent 125 sabotage groups totalling 3,364 men along with some 600 hastily recruited youths. Over the next few months they also sent 160 specially trained 'Organisers of Underground Work' to train and organise the partisans.

During 1942 the number of volunteers coming forward to join the partisans had drastically reduced. The poor war situation and the heavy toll inflicted on the early volunteers made few willing to get involved unless they were forced to do so. This lack of enthusiasm led to the introduction of conscription, which was highly unpopular with the Russian peasants. Red Army enforcers would often take hostages to make sure the conscripted members of their families did not desert. At the same time the German occupiers were rounding up Russian civilians and sending them to work as slave labourers. They were often forced to leave their children behind which was often a death sentence for the helpless youngsters, who died of starvation. Brutal treatment of the population by the Germans, however, served as a 'recruiting sergeant' for the partisans, with the peasants having little to lose. By December 1942 there were an estimated 130,000 partisans with 57,000 in Belorussia, 20,000 in the Smolensk region and 24,000 in the Bryansk region.

The other 30,000 were spread out between the Baltic states, Ukraine, Crimea and the Caucasus. Ukraine was never a fertile place for the partisans to fight, and in the early days the Communist Party was ordered to send 33,000 of its members into the vast territory. Their instructions were to bolster the existing partisans and give the movement there some organisation. However, despite Soviet propaganda the reality was that the Ukrainians were hostile to the outsiders. Few of these men and women survived for long with many being betrayed to the Germans by the local population. Despite the early setbacks the partisans were able to take control of some areas of occupied Russia and establish 'partisan' regions – *partizanskie kraya*. These were established in areas where the advance of the Axis forces had been so swift that large regions were left without any real German authority. Much of Belorussia and Northern Ukraine were heavily forested, which allowed the partisans to survive. Despite the lack of support from the local population in the early months of the occupation they were able to expand their armed detachments. The Germans and their Axis allies simply did not have the manpower to completely control other regions like Bryansk and Orel Province. Partisans, along with left behind Soviet officials, were able to fill the vacuum and act as the de-facto government over vast areas. Orel Province had at least 18,000 active partisans in fifty-four detachments who controlled 500 villages, and by the winter of 1942–43, 50 per cent of Belorussia was in partisan hands. The early months of the German occupation were hard for the long-suffering Soviet population to bear. In reality many Russians were not supporters of the Stalin regime, but the harsh treatment by the occupiers soon turned the people against the invaders.

(**Left**) Four Militiamen pose in the suburbs of the Ukrainian city of Kharkov in 1941 during the German attack from 20 to 24 October. In the early months of the German invasion the civilian resistance was poorly organised. These men who will soon become partisans are relatively well armed with three having Mosin-Nagant M1891 rifles as well as Nagant revolvers and plenty of grenades. (*Author's Collection*)

(**Opposite, above**) Factory workers parade at the start of the German invasion of the Soviet Union in the summer of 1941 armed with whatever rifles were available. In urban areas most fighters joined militia rather than partisan units, but if a city or town fell to the Germans these men and women could become irregulars in the countryside. The banner behind the volunteers says celebrate the anniversary of the Glorious October Revolution! (US National Archives)

Soviet propaganda always portrayed older
partisans like this man with a full beard as the
backbone of the anti-German resistance. They
were often veterans of the Russian Civil War of
1917–22 and brought their experience to their
comrades. Older men, however, were often more
cynical of the way they had been treated by the
authorities in the early days of partisan resistance.
Often left without support, some experienced
partisans were resentful about the lack of military
aid they received from Moscow. They were, of
course, more angry about the way their country
was being laid waste by the invader and continued
to fight to the end. (*Author's Collection*)

A happy group of partisans show off their weaponry to a propaganda photographer in 1942. Using a wide variety of small arms and machine guns of course led to the usual problems of replacing ammunition once the captured rounds had run out. Thousands of PPSH-41 submachine guns were air dropped to the partisans along with boxes of ammunition by Red Air Force aircraft. (*Author's Collection*)

This officer of the partisans has an air of experience and authority about him and he may well have served in the Red Army in 1941. Officers in charge of left-behind units during the summer of 1941 were expected to organise their men into partisan units. Life as a partisan commander could be precarious, and those who were deemed not to be as enthusiastic as they should be could be replaced and shot without warning. (*Author's Collection*)

This partisan commander has no sign of
rank on his uniform and only has the five
pointed red star on his fur hat as insignia.
The only indication of his status is the smart
great coat and his general air of superiority
and toughness. Partisan commanders
were supposed to lead by example
when necessary and they had to answer
constantly to their superiors and political
officers especially if a mission failed without
a viable excuse. (*Author's Collection*)

As was often the case with partisan bands,
a young volunteer has been paired with a
more mature comrade who fires a Madsen
light machine gun. His young comrade is
ready with another curved magazine which
came in twenty-five-, thirty- or forty-round
versions for this Danish designed weapon.
These guns had originally been bought by
the Imperial Russian Army in 1908 and
would have been put into storage until
needed again in 1941. (*Author's Collection*)

A column of horse carts carry a large partisan unit over the open countryside with their rifles and machine guns at the ready. This way of travelling was of course very risky as long as the Luftwaffe had planes in the sky that could easily strafe the men. These men look fairly relaxed so perhaps they are far enough from an enemy airfield or airstrip to give them some reassurance. Some partisan-controlled regions were marked in red on the maps of the Luftwaffe as being areas to avoid due to heavy anti-aircraft ground fire. (*Author's Collection*)

This poignant image shows the types of ages of the partisan fighters taking part in the anti-Axis war with a 'grandfather' and a boy who may well be his grandson. Both fighters are armed with the standard Mosin-Nagant M1891 rifle and the boy appears to be wearing the Red Army padded jacket. With most partisans wearing civilian clothing, any male captured in a warzone could expect in most cases to be shot or hanged by their captors. (*Author's Collection*)

Three resolute looking partisans pose with their PPSH-41 submachine guns held proudly on their chests. Although many partisans were older, or were young men and boys, these three will probably be sent to join the Red Army if possible. When the first partisan groups were formed they were made up largely of army stragglers, escaped prisoners of war and communist activists and officials. (*Author's Collection*)

Two younger partisans have been issued with winter clothing by their unit, or may have brought their own coats and hats from home. Both youths have sewn a piece of red cloth to the front of their civilian fur hats as was common among the Soviet partisans. It was also common to carry bandoliers of bullets over each shoulder to keep the units machine guns supplied. (*Author's Collection*)

A group of Belorussian partisans in 1942 celebrate a victory at their base in the forests which covered the region. This unit appears to be well armed with SVT-40 automatic rifles carried by several of the men in the background. The fighter in the foreground is armed with a DT-29 light machine gun which were usually mounted in tanks. When necessary the machine gun could be dismounted and used as an infantry support weapon. (*Author's Collection*)

This dramatically posed photograph of Soviet partisans in action shows the man in the foreground holding a PPSH-41 submachine gun with a seventy-one-round drum magazine on it. In front of him on the ground he has a spare pair of thirty-round curved magazines for his PPSH. The partisan in the centre of the group has a SVT-40 semi-automatic rifle which was in widespread use as the war went on. Some recruits to the partisans were young men who had been called to the colours but due to the confusion of the German invasion had not been able to get to their training camps. (*Author's Collection*)

These partisans in the Smolensk region have been liberally supplied with enough PPSH-41 submachine guns to arm most of their group. The Soviet submachine gun was being produced in huge numbers and this cheap but serviceable weapon was ideal for the kind of 'hit and run' fighting partisans took part in. (*Author's Collection*)

A group of partisans in the Leningrad region are seen on parade with various insignia on their fur hats. The man in the foreground has chosen to sew a large red star onto his hat to make sure his allegiance is clear. He is the officer in charge of a reconnaissance patrol and has a map case, a compass and a pair of binoculars. Interestingly, he is armed with a captured German Bergman MP35 submachine gun which was the predecessor to the MP40. (*Author's Collection*)

(**Above, left**) This young partisan has a veritable arsenal around his waist as he poses for the camera in a break from fighting in 1942. Besides his PPSH-41 submachine gun he has what look like two Nagant M1895 revolvers, one in a holster and the other tucked into his belt. His grenades come in various makes with RGD-33 tucked into his belt and a RG-14/30 hanging on his right hip. The three pineapple type grenades are F1s, which were based on the French F1 and the larger grenade is an unknown type with a larger explosive charge. (*Author's Collection*)

(**Above, right**) This happy woman partisan known only as 'Natya' has been rewarded for her bravery by being given a prized MP-38 submachine gun by her comrades. Whether fighting at the front line or acting as nurses, spies and saboteurs, the female partisans suffered heavily. As many photographs and written records show, if anything women and girl partisans were treated more harshly than their male comrades if captured. (*Author's Collection*)

(**Opposite, above**) Partisans of the 'Kletnyanskaya Brigade' march past their commander in the Smolensk region in 1944. Having begun as disorganised groups of fighters in 1941 and 1942, by the end of 1944 most larger partisan bands were acting as well organised military units. Even though most had a para-military uniform or wore their own clothes they were expected to turn up for parade in a reasonable state of dress. (*Author's Collection*)

(**Opposite, below**) Another view of the previous photograph shows the partisan leader watching from his horse as his Otrad marches past on the way out of a town at which they had stopped. In front of him is a version of the Russian Civil War *tachanka*, which is a cart with a Maxim M1910 machine gun mounted at the back. This mobile machine gun was successfully used by the Red Army especially the 1st Red Cavalry Army in the Russian Civil war. This version, however, is not pulled by cavalry horses it is pulled by farmers horses and the improvised *tachanka* is too large to be pulled at speed into battle. (*Author's Collection*)

A teenage girl milks a cow which is being kept in the partisan hideout in the forests of occupied Russia. When the partisans became stronger in numbers, feeding the fighters, especially in winter, became a major problem. Although the local population, whether through choice or coercion, often supplied the partisans with food. However, the harsh German punishments meted out to anyone who supported the partisans meant the peasant farmers were often reluctant to aid their compatriots. Of course, the partisans tried to be as self-sufficient as possible by keeping livestock when they felt secure in their forest bases. (*Author's Collection*)

This image of a young partisan machine gunner shows off the forty-seven-bullet pan magazine of the Degtyaryov DP27/DP-28 light machine gun to good effect. First issued in 1927, the Degtyaryov was the standard light machine gun of the Soviet Red Army until 1945 and beyond. Although improved in 1943 it was to serve the Soviet soldier well, even though it did have some faults. (*Author's Collection*)

Partisans operate a rare piece of artillery during the early fighting in 1941 with the period evidenced by the *budenovka* hat worn by one of the crew. The gun is a 76mm M1933 divisional gun which had entered service that year and served the Red Army until 1945 and beyond. In 1941 it was being replaced by the M1936 but any in partisan hands would have been put into their service. (*Author's Collection*)

This determined-looking female partisan is E.I. Kulesh of the 'People's Avenger' brigade, which was operating around the city of Minsk in 1942. She holds a Mosin-Nagant rifle and has a red army F-1 pineapple grenade attached to her belt which had been introduced into service in 1939. (*Author's Collection*)

A cheerful 15-year-old partisan, Misha Petrov, is pictured in a forest camp armed with a captured MP-38 submachine gun and an RGD-33 grenade tucked into his boot. The photograph was taken in Belarus in 1943, the main centre for partisan activity in the occupied Soviet Union. (*Author's Collection*)

A Soviet military instructor parachutes out of a Red Air Force Li-2 transport, the licence made version of the US DC-3. As the partisan forces developed it became apparent that many units – Otrads – were short of military experts so some were sent to help them. In particular demand were explosives experts and communications experts who could train the more capable partisans. Many of these experts had little or no parachuting experience which must have led to a high attrition rate during the operation. (*Author's Collection*)

An ex-Red Air Force Polikarpov I-15 fighter is being used by the partisans to supply their forces. This out-of-date plane, which was introduced in the mid-1930s, could still perform as a useful liaison aircraft between partisan groups. It could also be used to deliver small amounts of arms and ammunition and other vital supplies to the isolated units. To keep the I-15 safe from air attack the partisans are camouflaging it until its needed to go on another mission. (*Author's Collection*)

This poster depicting a partisan destroying a telephone line has the caption 'Glory to the Hero partisans destroying the Fascist's Rear'. The Soviet people not under occupation were told that the partisans were making life impossible for the occupying powers and their collaborators. (*Author's Collection*)

Old peasant men like this partisan 'grey beard' found themselves having to go to war again often having served in earlier conflicts going back to the Russo-Japanese War of 1904–05. Some would be able to bring their basic military training to good use in helping the young men and boys learn how to handle rifles. Many, like this man, would be issued with a Mosin-Nagant M1891, which was one of the standard rifles used in the war with Japan. One old partisan, called Korenev, featured in the Soviet press and was known by the affectionate name 'Grandfather Frost' after a Russian fairytale character. (*Author's Collection*)

Two partisans fire from cover towards German positions armed with a captured MG-34 machine gun and a Red Army Mosin-Nagant M1891 carbine. The loader is feeding the belt of bullets through the MG-34 while keeping his carbine ready to give the firer covering fire. (*Author's Collection*)

This well-armed partisan unit bristling with weaponry is seen in the morning light at their forest base in Belorussia. Besides the Soviet weaponry they have a ZB-30 light machine gun, which was first made in Czechoslovakia in the early 1930s. This weapon could have been captured from the Germans, Slovaks and Romanians who all used it during the war. (*Author's Collection*)

A demolition squad clamber over the abutment supporting the tracks of a high level railway line. This kind of stone-built support would require a great deal of explosive to destroy it, which would take a long time to lay correctly. The longer they worked the more likely they were to be discovered by the constant patrols moving up and down the lines. It was reported, however, that during the partisan war they were able to destroy 1,600 bridges, and from September to November 1943 they damaged 20,505 rails. (*Author's Collection*)

A partisan lights the fuse on an explosive charge before taking cover and waiting for the arrival of a German train. This fighter is probably the leader of a small sabotage unit and has claimed a German MP-40 submachine gun as his personal weapon. Any German or auxiliary Russian troops who tried to defuse the explosives would come under fire from this partisan and his comrades. (*Author's Collection*)

A partisan sabotage group, having despatched a guard, are now rushing to lay their charges along the railway line before other guards turn up. The forest that had provided them with cover once they left the embankment has been cut down to make sure that they will be exposed while they go about their work. (*Author's Collection*)

Belorussian partisans move through a marsh as they try to avoid meeting any Axis troops in the open. German maps often designated these marshes as impassable, but of course local knowledge meant that the safe paths through them could be found. Partisans did suffer losses while moving across terrain like this but with guides they stood a better chance of crossing them than their German pursuers. (*Author's Collection*)

A long column of Belorussian partisans march through along the edge of a forest during the summer of 1942. The men are a real mixture of soldiers, militia and civilians who have volunteered to fight the invaders. Every type of headgear is being worn by the men, with winter fur hats worn alongside peaked caps and civilian flat caps, while one man wears the now out of date *budenovka* hat with pointed crown. (*Author's Collection*)

Children were often involved with the partisans mainly in menial roles, and asked to carry arms only in extreme circumstances. Boys and girls often acted as spies for the partisans as they were supposed to be inconspicuous, but it was dangerous work. As the Germans became more wary, these spies and informants were often uncovered and were usually executed like their adult comrades. (*Author's Collection*)

This photograph shows Sidor Kovpak a veteran of the Russian Civil War 1917–1922 who later became a school teacher. During the Second World War he became a prominent partisan commander leading 10,000 men in the Ukraine and having the luxury of a number of field guns. These were positioned at his HQ at Putivt and helped keep anti-partisan forces at bay. As the German Army retreated Kovpak's men destroyed much of the rail infrastructure they needed to transport their men. (*Author's Collection*)

A partisan sentry stands guarding his base HQ armed with a Steyr MP-34 submachine gun. This German-made gun was used mainly in Russia by SS and police units instead of the MP-38 and MP-40. Its high quality manufacture made it expensive to produce and it would have been a rare sight in a partisan armoury. (*Author's Collection*)

Belorussian partisan fighter Alena Ostapovna Ataman, with her daughter Marusya in her arms, is ready to fight to protect her two daughters. When the Russians were faced with death, either by starvation or by execution, they had little choice but to fight. Alena is armed with a Mosin-Nagant M1891 rifle which she may or may not have a chance to practice with. (*Author's Collection*)

This partisan in the Caucasus Mountains, Shota Sholamberidze, is armed with a PPSH-41 submachine gun. On his back he has the weight of a metal bipod for a 107 mm mortar – the GVPM 1938. His headdress is Caucasian and he appears to be wearing a Red Army greatcoat to keep him warm on a cold night in the mountains.

A Soviet paratrooper has dropped behind enemy lines, probably in the Caucasus, to issue local partisans with instructions. He pores over a map of the region while the two partisans try to take in the information he is giving them. Military experts who were sent to join the partisans added greatly to the effectiveness of the various units they helped. Many partisan leaders proved incapable of dealing with some of the more sophisticated aspects of military science. (*Author's Collection*)

A partisan officer looks out from horseback for any enemy movements through his military issue binoculars. There were small mounted units among the partisans but cavalry horses were usually reserved for the many Red Army Cavalry and Cossack units. From photographic evidence it appears that the commander of a partisan unit and some of his officers were often mounted when horses were available. (*Author's Collection*)

An unknown girl partisan poses for the camera with a carbine over her left shoulder and a belt of machine gun ammunition over her right. The most famous female partisan was Zoya Kosmodemyanskaya, who died in action in 1942. She was posthumously awarded the title 'Hero of the Soviet Union' to encourage her fellow Russians to make the same sacrifices as she had. (*Author's Collection*)

Chapter Three

German Partisan Operations 1941-1944

The lightning advance into Russia by the Germans in June 1941 eventually and inevitably slowed in the autumn and early winter. 'Operation Barbarossa' was to continue for five months from 22 June 1941 until 8 December. This startling advance had left large areas of western and central Russia in German hands, along with millions of Soviet citizens left behind by the retreating Red Army. In the Baltic and Ukraine the Germans were often enthusiastically welcomed by the population. It was now a moment of truth as the population of the above regions and Belorussia looked for favourable treatment by the occupiers. Any hope of exploiting the friendly welcome from much of the Russian population was quashed when the Nazi's harsh policies against Eastern people became apparent. German intentions towards the Russian population and their plans to deal with any opposition were made clear just a month after Barbarossa began.

In a directive of 25 July 1941 the OKH – Oberkommando des Heeres (High Command of the German Army) cautioned their soldiers against any 'soft' treatment of the Russian population. A few months later Field Marshal Keitel told his troops to regard any opposition to their occupation with brutality saying that fifty to a hundred Russians should be shot for every German soldier killed by partisans. Harsh policies like this totally failed to exploit the genuine opposition to the Soviet regime in many areas of occupied Russia, especially in Ukraine. Much of the anti-partisan campaign was left to the rear units of the German divisions fighting at the front line in Russia. These units forcibly deported hundreds of thousands of Russians to work as slave labourers in Germany. They also looted the local villages and towns which held the reserves from Soviet agricultural production, which were supposed to feed the population over the severe winter. Not surprisingly, the peasants resisted the confiscation of their crops, which meant that thousands of their population would die of starvation in 1941–42. The growth of partisan groups during 1941 and the following year was met by a level of brutality by the Germans that was difficult to comprehend. In September 1941 an article in a German magazine summed up the attitude of many Germans during their anti-partisan campaigns in Europe in the Second World War. It said:

> Insurrectional movements have arisen in German occupied territory … We must undertake without delay the most rigorous measures to affirm the authority of the occupying power and to avoid an extension of these attacks. We must never lose sight of the fact that, in occupied countries, a human life is worth less than nothing and that intimidation is only possible through extraordinarily harsh measures. When taking reprisals for the death of a German soldier, the execution of 50 to 100 Communists is essential … The method of execution should reinforce yet more the impact of the punishment.

In late October 1942 a rabidly anti-Jewish German officer Erich von dem Bach-Zelewski was given the role of SS Plenipotentiary against the partisans. By December he had a staff whose role was to implement a campaign of terror against both partisans and anyone who sympathised with them. Some Wehrmacht officers serving on the Eastern Front did not agree with the brutal policy and saw it as counterproductive. One senior officer, General Strik-Strikfeldt, was quoted as saying: 'rather a little more psychology and a little less blood'. Hitler did not agree at all with this sentiment and said that the only successful anti-partisan operations were those where the utmost brutality was used against the population.

During 1942 and 1943, large-scale encirclement operations were the norm which often included utilising German regular army units withdrawn from the front line. These operations involved the destruction of villages which were suspected of supporting the partisans. Some soldiers may have seen these operations of a break of sorts from the bitter fighting at the front, but it was hard work both physically and emotionally. It would be a hard-hearted soldier who was unmoved by the extermination of the populations of these villages – men, women and children. Four of the main encirclement operations were: 'Operation Bamberg' – 26 March to 6 April 1942; 4,396 'partisans' killed for a loss of seven Germans killed! 'Operation Hanover' – April to June 1942, which saw 45,000 Germans battling 20,000 partisans and losing 2,200 men, while the partisans lost over 10,000 men. In July 1942 'Operation Vogelsang' resulted in the deaths of 1,193 partisans, with the Germans suffering fifty-eight killed and 138 wounded. 'Operation Zigeunerbaron' – May to June 1943 was intended to disrupt the partisan activity in support of the Red Army fighting at the six-week-long Battle of Kursk – early July until late August. During 'Operation Kottbus' in Belorussia in 1943, a total of 4,500 'fighters' were killed but many of the dead were identified as women and children. The Germans claimed to have captured 492 rifles but did not explain what threat the civilians had been to their anti-partisan operation.

When the Germans attacked a village and indiscriminately killed men, women and children, the victims had to be listed as 'partisans' and later as 'bandits'. This led to what was called the 6,000/480 problem, with 6,000 civilians killed and listed as partisans but only 480 weapons captured. In addition, the low casualty rate among the German soldiers made the claim that they had faced partisan resistance unbelievable. On some operations which killed several thousand 'armed' bandits, the casualty rate was listed as '0 per cent'.

It was not until autumn 1944 that the Germans issued a practical guide to fighting the partisans called 'On Fighting Bands'. This guide emphasised that the fighting against the partisans should not be seen as a 'second-rate fight'. It required the best troops to deal with the enemy and they should be well trained and totally committed to their task. As the Red Army advanced through Russia and then Poland in 1944, the anti-partisan fight became largely irrelevant to the Germans. The partisan war was a constant drain on German resources and the impending defeat caused some high ranking officials to reflect. In the latter stages of the partisan war in Russia, the SS Leader Heinrich Himmler made a rather measured and telling statement. He said, without an hint of irony: 'Perhaps we have overreacted to these bandits, and by this have caused ourselves needless problems.'

(**Opposite, above**) A German Army Hotchkiss H-35 tank formerly of the French Army moves through a burning Russian village during an anti-partisan sweep in the winter of 1942–43. Tanks like this were not really battle-worthy by this period of the war and were passed onto German security units to use in their operations. These types of anti-partisan operations did nothing to win any kind of 'hearts and minds' policy, which by 1943 did not exist anyway. (*Author's Collection*)

(**Opposite, below**) During an anti-partisan operation a squad of German soldiers enters a village under the cover of a Soviet BT-7 tank which was brought back into action after its capture in the early stages of the war. The Germans would search in the wooden houses for hidden partisans or weapons and any other supplies which had been secreted. The 'suspect' population of the village or hamlet would often be made up of old people and women and children. Their fates were in the hands of the Germans and the least they could expect was to see their homes in flames and their livestock killed or confiscated. (*Author's Collection*)

A German soldier moves warily into a house with his Luger 1908 pistol at the ready while his comrades cover him from behind. Any suspect man or woman found hiding would be either be interrogated in front of their fellow villagers or taken to the unit HQ. The end result for any suspect was usually execution, and further consequences for their village. (*Author's Collection*)

Anti-partisan troops, according to a German 1944 guide to fighting bandits, should be: 'particularly agile and cunning' and 'hardened and frugal'. This German soldier suspects that partisans may be hiding in the roof of a village barn and peers into the darkness, looking and listening for signs of life. After anyone was taken away for questioning the family of the suspect were removed from their home and it was set alight. The villagers would then be warned that any further signs of support for the partisans would see the whole of the village burnt to the ground. (*Author's Collection*)

(**Above**) German Army officers pore over a map looking for any areas where partisan activity was reported. Many villagers were not in full support of the partisans and German reports said that farmers would travel as far as twelve miles to give information to them. As in most conflicts the ordinary family or village just wanted to be left alone by all sides, but this was seldom the case. They were caught between the 'wrath' of both partisans and occupiers it was the ordinary peasant who suffered on most occasions. (*Author's Collection*)

(**Right**) The radio operator of a Waffen SS unit keeps in touch with his headquarters while his comrades take a break during an anti-partisan operation in 1942. During that year the Waffen SS took over responsibility for coordinating anti-partisan operations from the Wehrmacht. The SS personnel were expected to be less squeamish when it came to dealing with the Russian population. Some historians estimate that about a million Russians were killed during the course of these operations. (*Author's Collection*)

(**Above, left**) German troops prepare to move forward during an anti-partisan operation through a forest that shows the aftermath of a German bombardment. The SS were particularly active in operations against the Soviet partisans and often dealt with civilian men and youths as 'bandits'. One such SS operation in early 1942, code-named 'Marsh Fever', had a toll of 389 partisans shot, 1,274 suspected partisans shot, and as an afterthought it was mentioned that 8,350 Jews had been 'liquidated'. (*Author's Collection*)

(**Above, right**) An unspecified 'foreign' volunteer of the German Army waits to go on an anti-partisan patrol in 1943. One of the main mistakes made by the Germans in Russia and its various republics was in not harnessing the real dislike of many of the peoples of the Soviet Union to their government. The Soviet Union was full of people who had suffered at the hands of the Stalinist regime and many were willing to fight against their former leader. (*Author's Collection*)

(**Opposite**) German Wehrmacht troops rest during an anti-partisan operation with the faces showing the strain of this kind of warfare. The Nazis noted that the brutal treatment meted out to the Russian population did take a toll on the men who were ordered to take part. Some army commanders did their best to mitigate the amount of brutality used but there was little even a high ranking Wehrmacht officer could do without facing his own consequences. (*Author's Collection*)

(**Above**) A group of Waffen SS troops gather in a forest clearing before moving out against their next objective during an anti-partisan sweep. The Russians should have expected the brutal treatment they received from the SS as they had already shown their brutality during the invasion and occupation of Poland. The Soviet Red Army had committed equally brutal acts during their occupation of Eastern Poland in 1939. They killed thousands of Polish intelligentsia in the period before Germany's Operation Barbarossa in June 1941 pushed them out of the country.(*Author's Collection*)

(**Opposite, above**) An SS patrol walk across a wooden walkway in a swampy region in Belorussia, with the lead man having an Erma EMP submachine gun. The ruthlessness of the SS in Russia were all part of the Nazi policy of the reduction in the Slav population from 1941. In early 1941 Heinrich Himmler had declared that the Slav population should be reduced by at least 30 million. Anti-partisan operations by the SS were part of the brutal policy, with the population of whole villages killed with the token excuse that they were all 'bandits'. (*Author's Collection*)

(**Opposite, below**) During an anti-partisan sweep in 1942, Russian volunteers armed with captured PPSH-41 submachine guns guard some prisoners. Russians chose to work with the Germans for varied reasons, with many choosing this rather than a slow death in a prison camp. Others genuinely hated the Soviet regime which had killed and imprisoned millions of Russians since 1918, some of which may have been these collaborators friends and relatives. (*Author's Collection*)

(**Above**) A lone German Army soldier looks out over the steppes of Ukraine, scanning for any partisan activity. In early 1941 the Wehrmacht had set up 'Security Divisions' to deal with securing the rear of the army and in carrying out anti-partisan operations. These units followed the rules used by Imperial powers in the nineteenth century, especially in Africa. A quote on the subject said that 'All resistance was regarded as illegitimate, and civilians were targeted pre-emotively and often collectively to forestall future resistance'. (*Author's Collection*)

(**Opposite, above**) This dishevelled looking suspected partisan is being interrogated in a Russian village in the summer of 1942. An interpreter asked questions put to him by the paratrooper Fallschirmjäger to his left. He is surrounded by other paratroopers and army personnel who presumably are there to intimidate him. Any information given under duress was often unreliable and the fate of the prisoner was probably known to him, giving him little incentive to cooperate. (*Author's Collection*)

(**Opposite, below**) SS panzer crewmen stop in a Russian village and ask for directions from one of the older residents. Of course, providing intelligence to the enemy would be a death sentence for any Russian civilian if the partisans found out. The constant dilemma for many peasants was that if the the partisans had not protected them from the invaders, what should they now do? Peasants often wanted to be left alone by all sides in the struggle for Soviet Russia, but usually they were punished by one side or the other. (*Author's Collection*)

(**Above**) These German troops are Jagdkommandos – their task was denoted by the hunting term *kesseltreiben* (witch hunt). The Jagdkommando units were designated to be no smaller than a platoon and no larger than a company in strength. They are questioning a captured partisan looking for information on the whereabouts of his comrades. In the build up to the Battle of Kursk in 1943 the Germans launched a series of five anti-partisan operations. During May and June these operations managed to kill a large number of partisans but did not stop those who survived from aiding their Red Army comrades when the battle began in July. By 1943 the partisans were becoming more important to the Red Army and they proved their worth over the next year. (*Author's Collection*)

(**Opposite, above**) Two SS officers humiliate their captives who are suspected of being partisans and are now roughly searched by their captors. The Asiatic appearance of the two 'partisans' will seal their fate regardless of any other factors as they are seen by the Germans as belonging to an inferior race. It is a curious paradox that the Waffen SS were willing to recruit 'certain' Asiatic men as the war progressed and they became more desperate for volunteers to fill their ranks. (*Author's Collection*)

(**Opposite, below**) This chilling photograph shows a group of young Waffen SS men gathering around a disabled Russian woman. In this photograph none of the men are mistreating the obviously confused woman, who tries to make conversation with the German with the SVT-40 automatic rifle. These men were, however, trained to show little or no mercy to anyone who showed defiance to their orders. Perhaps the state of mind of this poor woman may save her from execution but this was seldom the case when the SS were involved. (*Author's Collection*)

(**Above**) In their constant efforts to counter the attacks of Soviet partisans, the German Army in Russia often had to improvise. This mounted anti-partisan unit was photographed in the summer of 1942 when the threat against the occupiers was at its highest. This unit is hiding in the forests where their partisan enemies were usually taking shelter and are well armed with submachine guns and MG34 machine guns. (*Author's Collection*)

(**Opposite, above**) German troops move cautiously through marshland on the Crimean Peninsula towards partisan forces in 1943. The NCO in the lead of the patrol is armed with an MP-38 submachine gun a model which was produced in much smaller numbers than the later MP-40. After the conquest of the Crimea, the occupation in October 1941 was administered by Erich von Manstein's 11th Army. The Germans received some support from the Tartar population who were largely anti-Soviet with many volunteering to serve as auxiliaries in the Wehrmacht. (*Author's Collection*)

(**Opposite, below**) An SS Officer orders a family of Russian peasants to destroy the rifles from a cache of arms found in their house. The Mosin-Nagant M1891 rifles may have been forced on the family to hide and they will now pay heavily for being found in possession of them. In June 1943 the Germans launched an operation in Belorussia which resulted in the deaths of 9,500 'partisans'. When the captured weapons were counted it was found that there was a total of 492 rifles, which indicated how many of the total dead were in fact combatants. (*Author's Collection*)

(**Above, left**) A woman partisan who looks resigned to her fate is led away by her SS captives to be executed after an interrogation. The stoicism of the Soviet population during the German invasion and occupation was largely based on years of harsh rule under Stalin. They were used to surviving under a dictatorship but at the same time their patriotism for 'Mother Russia' was stronger than any opposition to Stalin. (*Author's Collection*)

(**Above, right**) The age or sex of anyone suspected of fighting for the partisans or aiding them in their fight against the German invaders offered little or no protection from punishment. This old man has been arrested and tied to a post by the Germans for interrogation, or possibly just for swift execution. Most partisans captured in populated areas were hanged or shot publicly to make an example of them to the population. (*Author's Collection*)

(**Opposite, above**) German troops are either removing charges placed under the railway sleeper or are placing some themselves. As the war progressed, at times the Germans had to resort to destroying track that could be used by the advancing Red Army. They did not like to be left exposed during this kind of activity and one soldier has his rifle over his shoulder while a comrade is ready to give covering fire from his MG-34 machine gun. (*Author's Collection*)

(**Opposite, below**) The crew of a German armoured train peer into the distance across the Russian steppes looking for any possible threats from partisan attacks. Just out of view is the light anti-aircraft gun which protects the train from attacks, but the armour on the turret shows that it has been damaged in a previous encounter. Although these gigantic trains were imposing they were still susceptible to mines and explosions on the railway tracks laid by partisans. (*Author's Collection*)

A German unit are aboard a captured Russian armoured train which is protected by a Type 'O' armoured locomotive and a two-turret artillery car. The infantry are protected behind double walls of cast concrete which can have sandbags added to create shooting positions. At the front of the infantry cars is a 37mm anti-tank gun to give the train more firepower when attacked by partisans. (*Author's Collection*)

A well armed German armoured train moves along a railway line at full steam with a crewman of the 105mm gun in the artillery car looking out for enemy movement. The train has been covered in foliage and tree branches in an effort to camouflage it from air attack. Although these trains were mobile fortresses they had their limitations and were dependent on undamaged track or they became virtual sitting ducks for audacious partisan attacks. (*Author's Collection*)

A smartly turned out German railwayman of the German State Railways, Deutsche Reichbahn, is wearing the dark blue uniform in Russia in 1942. This uniform dated back to the pre-1933 Weimar Republic and stayed the same after 1941 apart from the Nazi collar insignia. As a non-military organisation there were no military ranks, but there was a bewildering system of what was classified as 'Workers Classifications' which showed the wearer's status. Reichbahn personnel may officially have been civilians but they were expected to bear arms to protect their trains from partisan attacks. He has been issued with a Mauser rifle to protect the train after being given some rudimentary training. (*Author's Collection*)

(**Above**) As the situation in Russia deteriorated the men of the Deutsche Reichbahn were expected to fight alongside security police and local Russian volunteers. Railway operating units, Feldeisenbahn-Direktion (Field Railway Direction, or FED) were formed by Major-General Gercke. Each Army Group in Russia had a FED unit which was formed from drafted railwaymen led by German Army officers. These FED men, wearing the dark blue uniform, are manning a machine gun post which is part of the defensive system set up to counter partisan attacks on the railway. They have been issued with a captured Russian Maxim M1910 machine gun and Mauser rifles and are scouring the countryside looking for partisan activity. (*Author's Collection*)

(**Opposite**) This railwayman of the Feldeisenbahn-Direktion is stood in a lookout tower which appears to be guarding the goods yard of a Russian train station. Initially 25,000 German railwaymen had been sent to Russia, but the task they faced called for more manpower. As with the German Army in Russia, the only way to make up this shortfall was by recruiting Russian railway workers. There were at least 100,000 Russians recruited, but they would be suspected whenever sabotage took place. Most seconded railwaymen were older; this man appears to be younger and may well be drafted into the army in due course. He is wearing the field grey uniform of the Wehrmacht with the black and gold collar insignia of the FED and unidentified badges on his arm. Older arms were issued to second-line and security forces and this man has been given a Gewehr 98 rifle used by the German Army from 1898 until 1935. (*Author's Collection*)

Chapter Four

Soviet Partisan Warfare 1943-1944

After the lessons of the early failures of the Soviet partisans had been learnt, and from the summer of 1943, they had a more positive impact on the war effort. On 14 July the Supreme Military Command in Moscow ordered all partisan forces behind German lines to begin a campaign against the railway lines. They were to concentrate on the region around Orel and Bryansk, where a Soviet offensive was to be launched. These targeted objectives began to have a more profound impact on the fighting at the front lines. During 1943 partisan attacks had a major effect on the railway system, and 298 locomotives were destroyed in June alone. Among the notable partisan successes in the autumn of 1943 was the destruction of four supply trains in quick succession. One of the trains was loaded with vital Tiger heavy tanks destined for the hard-pressed German Army. The other trains were full of ammunition, which exploded and severely damaged the tracks and other infrastructure. During July 1943 the number of incidents on the railways in occupied Russia had reached 1,114 and a month later had risen to 1,392.

By the middle of 1943 an estimated 250,000 partisans were faced by 500,000 anti-partisan forces. Successful anti-insurgency warfare relied on a superiority in numbers of anti-partisan forces over the partisans of four to one. During 1943 and into 1944 the partisans became vital in the planning of the Soviet Red Army, and in the build up to the titanic battle at Kursk they launched numerous attacks on the German military infrastructure. This was also the case during the Soviet's summer offensive of 1944, when they attacked German railways and communications. Air support for the anti-partisan forces began to be reduced, largely due to the fact that large tracts of northern and central Russia were too dangerous to fly over. On the Luftwaffe's tactical maps there were increasingly more red patches added, which showed that ground fire would be too heavy to allow any meaningful strikes to be made. Partisan morale surged after the Red Army's victory at Stalingrad in early 1943 as the Russian public realised that the tide had turned. After 1943, fighting with the partisans was no longer a suicidal act as the embattled Axis forces began a slow retreat.

The role of the Soviet partisans began to be less important as the Red Army pushed the Axis forces westwards during 1944 and into 1945. Many partisans were recruited into 'destruction battalions', whose role was to pacify the newly liberated territories of any anti-Soviet elements. Others were recruited into special NKVD units to prosecute the 'war against banditry' in Ukraine, the Baltic States and other regions of the Soviet Union where the Germans had been welcomed in 1941; 40,000 Belorussian partisans were employed in the role of hunting down any German troops and collaborators who had been bypassed by the Red Army offensives.

Casualties suffered by both sides during the partisan war are hard to calculate, largely due to the exaggerated propaganda issued by the opponents. It is only possible to try and pick through the various figures with, for instance, the partisan losses for 1943–44 being estimated by the Germans at 147,055 dead, 90,904 captured and 7,402 deserters. German Army Group Centre, the largest military force on the Eastern Front, issued figures for their casualties between the months of May and September 1943. They were 902 German dead, 1,864 wounded and 202 missing, while their Hungarian allies lost 344 dead, 501 wounded and seventy-two missing. In addition, they listed the 'expendable' Russian auxiliaries losses as 758 dead, 788 wounded and 3,512 missing, including deserters. German post-war assessments said that the total losses suffered by their forces due to partisan activity were 50,000 killed. This figure was dwarfed by the losses suffered in combat by the Germans on the Eastern Front with a figure of 4 million being a probable under-estimation.

(**Above**) In the early days of the partisan struggle against the German invaders this young boy and his comrade fire towards enemy positions. They are fighting in Leningrad province while the city itself was under siege in one of the titanic struggles of the Second World War. While the young partisan is armed with the standard Mosin-Nagant M1891 rifle, the machine gun is a German MG08/15 probably captured by the Russians during the First World War. (*Author's Collection*)

(**Opposite, above**) This Maxim M1910 heavy machine gun crew were all reported to be Jews fighting alongside other partisans. It was hardly surprising that Jewish men and women were willing to fight and die against the German invaders. Some chose to form their own all-Jewish partisan groups but these were not usually accepted by the mainstream Soviet partisan organisation. Any smaller groups of anti-German fighters were usually voluntarily or forcibly absorbed into the larger non-Jewish units. (*Author's Collection*)

(**Opposite, below**) Partisans man a Soviet 45mm M1932 anti-tank gun in defence of a village in the summer of 1943. Artillery was not widely distributed to most partisan units and trained crews were hard to find, especially in the early days of Soviet resistance. The partisans would of course utilise any weaponry they could obtain, whether by capturing it or by being issued it by the Red Army. (*Author's Collection*)

(**Above, left**) This poster issued by the Soviet propaganda bureau tells the partisans to beat the enemy 'without mercy!'. Not all partisans were willing volunteers for the Soviet cause as they believed they had been caught between a 'rock and a hard place'. If they didn't resist the invaders they would be punished by the Soviet authorities, and if they did they would be punished by the Germans! (*Author's Collection*)

(**Above, right**) Partisans of the Federov Group use a Soviet 82mm mortar in defence of their village headquarters in 1943. This BM-37 mortar, which had been introduced into service in 1937, would be one of the heavier pieces of weaponry in partisan hands. The Federov Group was one of the largest groups at 60,000 strong and was under the command of Oleksiy Federov and Alexander Saburov. (*Author's Collection*)

(**Opposite, above**) This action photograph catches the moment a partisan commander snatches the MG-34 machine gun from the body of a fallen German soldier. He looks ahead to the enemy positions that he and the rest of his unit are attacking across an open field. This weapon will be well used by the partisans as long as ammunition for the MG-34 can also be retrieved from the battlefield. (*Author's Collection*)

A large Soviet partisan unit struggles through a flooded forest as they keep on the move to avoid anti-partisan forces sent to fight them. The man in the foreground has been given the dubious honour of carrying his partisan band's DShK 12.7mm M1938 heavy machine gun. With the barrel weighing 74lb it was a relatively light weapon to carry unmounted, but it was an ungainly length for moving through undergrowth. With a maximum firing range of 2,500 metres, these machine guns were effective against low-flying German aircraft. (*Author's Collection*)

(**Opposite, above**) A unit of partisan cavalry prepare to go on a mission, with a teenage girl probably serving as a nurse for the fighters. Although cavalry allowed more mobility for the partisans they were left more vulnerable as their horses needed feeding and stabling. The determination to resist the invaders is etched on the face of the young woman who appears to be unarmed. Her comrade is armed with the esteemed German MP-40, which was usually earmarked for partisan officers when captured. (*Author's Collection*)

(**Opposite, below**) A partisan cavalry unit 'liberates' the Ukrainian town of Ovruch in November 1943 as the population looks on. After years of Soviet subjugation and genocide of the population of Ukraine many welcomed the advancing Germans in 1941. During the war the Allies could not understand why loyal 'Russians' should be willing to support the invaders. They chose to ignore or forget the mass starvation and other outrages ordered by Stalin in the 1920s and 1930s in Ukraine. Ukrainians were fearful of the treatment they would receive from the returning Russian troops and any collaborators were dealt with swiftly by the Soviet regime. (*Author's Collection*)

These Crimean partisans were operating in the region around the port of Odessa and were using natural features such as caves as their hideouts. They also set up camps in the mountains and took shelter in quarries dug during Imperial rule. During 1942 and 1943 the partisans suffered terribly with little or no outside supplies and had to eat the carcasses of long-dead horses. There were some reports of cases of partisans resorting to cannibalism out of desperation. By November 1943 there were an estimated 8,000 surviving partisans operating in the Crimean Mountains, from where they attacked the railways and small German and Romanian garrisons. The head of the Crimean resistance was a man called Makrosov, who was a veteran of the fighting in Crimea in 1918. (*Author's Collection*)

(**Above**) A Russian regular soldier gives some Crimean partisans instruction in the handling of a captured German MP-38 submachine gun. At first the Crimean partisans struggled and they suffered a heavy loss when the Yalta partisan detachment was destroyed by Romanian forces in December 1941. With support coming from the government, the partisans had established thirty-four separate detachments by April 1942. By mid-July the same year there were a reported 2,217 partisans operating in the forest of the Crimea. (*Author's Collection*)

(**Opposite, above**) In the early morning light a Russian policeman who had chosen to work for the Germans as police chief of his home town is led to his trial after its liberation. Any official who refused to work for the Germans was virtually signing their own death warrant and that of their family. The only defence men like this had was that he was defending his own family from German punishment. This excuse, however, was seldom if ever accepted by the partisans as a reason for collaborating with the enemy. (*Author's Collection*)

(**Opposite, below**) Another Russian official or informant is about to be shot by the local partisan unit, including a woman fighter. Life under Stalin's brutal regime had always been hard and the 1930s saw millions of Russians killed or imprisoned, often for no reason. Regardless of people's genuine grievances against the Soviet regime pre-1941, every Russian was now expected to defend the 'glorious motherland' against the invaders. (*Author's Collection*)

(**Above, left**) Partisans take part in anti-aircraft training using their rifles and a DP-28 light machine gun to try to bring down enemy planes. One of the weapons most feared by the partisans was the Luftwaffe's JU-87 Stuka dive bomber, which although an outdated first-line aircraft was still deadly as an anti-insurgent bomber. (*Author's Collection*)

(**Above, right**) This middle-aged couple were shoemakers who led a band of partisans with some success despite their lack of military training. Sometimes the leaders of smaller partisan groups came from the most unlikely of backgrounds, although in this case the husband probably had some military training. His wife is armed with the standard PPSH-41 while he has a PPD-40 which was originally produced in 1934. (*Author's Collection*)

(**Opposite, above**) A Russian peasant woman, Maria Petrova, receives the thanks of a partisan commander as she sees three of her sons off to join the anti-Axis struggle in Belarus. Like many mothers in occupied and unoccupied Russia, whether or not she agrees with the Soviet policies, this lady has no option but to send her sons to war. Soviet propaganda extolled the virtues of mothers and wives who supported their menfolk in fighting for the motherland. (*Author's Collection*)

(**Opposite, below**) This group of Smolensk partisans belong to one of the larger and better organised groups under the command of cavalry general Belov, with a total of 15,000 men. It was made up local partisans like these fighters and a large number of parachutists who had been dropped behind German lines. They were attacked by a German force of 40,000 men under the command of General von dem Bach-Zelewski. By the time the operation had finished the Germans had lost 2,000 men, while the partisans had suffered heavier losses. The young woman and the man with the trilby hat with a red star on it appear to be leaders of this particular group as they both have revolvers in their belts as well as PPSH-41s. (*Author's Collection*)

Two young partisans dressed for the Russian winter stand guard against any German attacks against their unit. Even the Germans had to admit that fighters like these were 'bold and skilled', and that they were often 'self-sacrificing, enthusiastic and even fanatical'. German officials also admitted that the partisans were a major problem for them and that they had to improve their anti-partisan tactics. To the surprise of the Germans the partisan movement continued to fight well during the winter of 1941, despite the harsh conditions. (*Author's Collection*)

Two partisans defend their position on the bank of a small river with their Mosin-Nagant M1891 rifle and a Maxim M08/15 medium machine gun. Partisans avoided fire fights like this whenever possible as they needed to preserve ammunition. Their tactics involved ambushes, sabotage, assassination and raids on enemy garrisons rather than open fights where they were often outgunned. (*Author's Collection*)

Four Women partisans fighting alongside the Red Army are standing in the centre of the Belorussian capital, Minsk, on 3 July 1944. By 28 July Brest-Litovsk and Bialystok were also liberated and the Red Army had advanced to the pre-1941 border of the Soviet Union. The young women have a variety of Soviet weaponry and one of the group is armed with a French Lebel carbine. (*Author's Collection*)

This photograph is of 14-year-old partisan Scout Mikhail Khavday, who has been awarded a medal by his commander. He belongs to the Chernigov-Volynsk partisan detachment and his role in the unit would be to relay messages to and from headquarters. (*Author's Collection*)

A smiling Nurse of the 2nd Partisan Brigade, M. Dmitrieva is armed with the standard PPSH-41 submachine gun. Although her role within the unit is as a non-combatant she may well be called on to fight when the time comes. Judging by two of her comrades in the background, she appears to belong to one of the mounted partisan units. (*Author's Collection*)

This photograph features two of the women partisans who helped liberate the Crimea in May 1944. On 9 May the port of Sevastopol was taken from the Germans and the last pockets of resistance were eliminated by the 12th. The two women reflect the diverse population of the peninsula, with the older woman appearing to be from the Tartar population. Her younger, blonde comrade is definitely from the Russian population who emigrated to the Crimea during the Tsarist era. (*Author's Collection*)

Two partisan demolition experts, Grachav and Utenkov, prepare to be parachuted into a region of Russia where their expertise is required. They are heading to the Trans-Carpathian region in western Ukraine; one of the Soviet versions of the US C-47 transports seen in the background. The Dakota was produced by Lisunov as the Li-2 and was one of the main transport planes of the Soviet Air Force during the Second World War. Brave men like this would be given basic parachute training and the casualty rate during the descent would be high, especially in the rugged terrain in which they would be landing. (*Author's Collection*)

(**Above**) These Soviet partisans belong to the Moldovan resistance that fought the Romanian Army in the Transnistria region. Transnistria had been annexed from Romania by the Soviets in August 1940, when it was known as the 'Moldavian Soviet Republic'. The Romanian Army 'liberated' the region when they became allies of the Germans and took part in Operation Barbarossa. The Communist Party of Moldavia ordered the creation of a partisan force, but this struggled to develop due to opposition to the Soviet occupation between 1940 and 1941. (*Author's Collection*)

(**Opposite**) Four partisans are seen in their forest base in the early days of resistance to the Germans, and are dressed in donated uniforms and armed with the usual mix of Soviet and captured German weaponry. These men belong to the Belorussian partisans who in August 1941 had 231 detachments, joined by new forces, totalling 7,200, who had arrived from unoccupied Soviet territory. Until March 1942 these fighters had to survive without much outside support and often with little support from the population. (*Author's Collection*)

(**Above**) These Jewish partisans belong to the Bielski Otred, a group of survivors of the pogroms in Belarus in 1941. The partisans were led by four brothers: Tuvia, Alexander (Zus), Aron and Asael, with the older brother Tuvia taking overall command. They rescued civilians from the ghettos in their area and after two years the group totalled 1,236 people. Only a small number fought as partisans while the rest lived in the camp in the Naliboki Forest. Initially, the fighting element of the Bielski partisans had only a handful of armed fighters, but the average number of armed partisans was about 125. When they became affiliated with the nearby Soviet partisans in 1943, they were forced to split their fighters into two: one group with 180 men and women, and another with 160 fighters. (*Author's Collection*)

(**Opposite, above**) This group of Jewish partisans joined the Soviet partisans having fled from one of the ghettos set up in Eastern Europe to house Jews until they could be 'dealt with'. Up to 30,000 Jews fought mostly within Russian and Belorussian Otrods (units), but some did form their own distinct groups. The main problem for independent Jewish units was the acute shortage of arms as they received little support from the other resistance groups. This meant they tended to undertake sabotage operations against railways and other infrastructure with only a few having rifles, or even just pistols. (*Private Collection*)

(**Opposite, below**) These Jewish fighters belong to the 'Fareynikte Partizaner Organizatsye', which was organised in the Vilna Ghetto in Lithuania. Two of its members: the woman on the far right, Vitka Kempner, and the man in the centre of the back row, Abba Kovner, married in 1946. The ghetto, which housed about 55,000 Jews, was run by the Nazis and by 1943 all but a few hundred of the population had died or been executed. Regular round ups of the population, starting with the old and those unable to work, ended in mass shootings followed by temporary lulls. In September 1943 the Germans decided to clear the ghetto entirely and sent the remaining Jews to the Vaivara concentration camp. Those who managed to escape from the ghetto tried to join local partisan groups, but these fighters had formed their own 'Jewish' group armed with Soviet and German submachine guns. (*Author's Collection*)

The survivors of the Vilna Ghetto in Vilnius that belonged to the FPO escaped into the Rudnikai Forest where they continued to fight the Germans. Here is Abba Kovner (with the long hair) and a fellow partisan in Vilnius. Kovner became a famous Israeli poet after the war when he moved to the new Jewish homeland. He was also well known for his extreme views on what would be a fit revenge on the German nation for the Holocaust. His political views called for the killing of 6 million Germans and he and his co-conspirators in the 'Nakam' (Revenge) group planned to poison the water supply to German cities. (*Author's Collection*)

Taras-Bulba-Borovets (1908–1981) – or officially, Taras Dmytrovych Borovets – was a Ukrainian resistance fighter in Ukraine during the Second World War. His nom-de-guerre was taken from the famous Cossack leader made famous by the novel of Nikolai Gogol. In 1941–42 he had formed a non-political unit of resistance fighters who were equally opposed to the German invaders as they were to the Soviet Red Army. Bulba-Borovet's small guerrilla group was absorbed by the Ukrainian People's Army which grew to about 200,000 men by 1944. (*Author's Collection*)

A Ukrainian People's Army officer stands in his forest base wearing the standard uniform worn by the UPA during the Second World War. The cap had been adapted with the distinctive V-shaped front which sometimes had the blue and yellow insignia of the UPA added. (*Author's Collection*)

These fighters of the Ukrainian People's Army pose with their captured German and Soviet submachine guns in a forest clearing in Western Ukraine in 1944. Shortages of small arms was a major problem for the Ukraine resistance with no reliable outside sources of weaponry. When photographs were taken the guerrillas were careful to put their best weaponry to the front to disguise the general lack of modern arms. The four men at the front of the group are armed with the following submachine guns from left to right: a Soviet PPS, a German MP-40, a German Bergman and a Soviet PPSH-41. (*Author's Collection*)

Male and female fighters of the Ukrainian People's Army take part in a religious festival in their forest base in 1944. The hard-pressed Ukrainian partisans fought the Germans, the Red Army and the Polish AK (Krajawa Armia). This group have captured a number of Soviet PPSH-41 and PPS submachine guns and a German MP-40. The young woman in the centre of the group appears to be unarmed and is probably a nurse or unit administrator. (*Author's Collection*)

Chapter Five

Axis Anti-Partisan Forces in Russia 1941–1944

In the early days of the German occupation the policy was not to employ 'friendly' Russians, including prisoners of war, in any military role. Individual German commanders, however, saw these Russians, Ukrainians and Baltic prisoners as an answer to their severe shortage of manpower. The first volunteer units raised in Russia were small in number and volunteers were recruited on a local basis by individual German officers. Many were recruited from among the desperate Russian prisoners of war dying by the thousand through starvation and neglect in German camps. Known by the Germans as Hilfswilligen (Volunteer Helpers), the most trusted of these volunteers were issued with rifles and stood guard. Others worked as drivers, store keepers and general labourers who were usually hoping to be given a rifle eventually. Captured uniforms and rifles were handed out to the 'Hiwis', as they became known, and white or yellow armbands were issued. By the spring of 1942 there were an estimated 200,000 Russians in German Army service and this number rapidly expanded to about a million by the end of the year. All this was done without the official sanction of Hitler or high-ranking officers, who chose to turn a blind eye to the practice. Manpower shortages meant that the role of the Hiwi was becoming more and more vital to the German war effort on the Eastern Front. On 6 November 1941 Himmler gave orders that all indigenous Auxiliary Police were to be formed into units known as Schutzmannschaften (Protection Squads), which was abbreviated to 'Schuma Btl'. Baltic, Belorussian and Ukrainian recruits were given German uniforms and ex-Soviet small arms. They were signed up on six-month rolling contracts but any disobedience or unsatisfactory performance often led to a bullet in the back of the head. Within the Schuma formations there were two types of unit, the Wachbataillon (Guard Battalions) and the Front Bataillon (Front Battalions). The Wachbataillon personnel were given local security and guard duties, while the Front Bataillon volunteers were to be sent on search and destroy operations. In total there were 200 Schuma Battalions with twenty-one made up of Estonians, forty-seven of Latvians, twenty-six of Lithuanians, eleven Belorussians, seventy-one Ukrainians and eight Tartars. Each Battalion had an average of 500 men but there was a great deal of variation in the individual unit strengths.

Heavily involved in the Eastern Front were the Einsatzgruppen (Deployment Groups) who were responsible for the killing of Jews and other 'undesirables' targeted by the Nazis. They had been formed in 1939 and first came to the fore during the occupation of Poland in September. Besides the Jewish population they killed members of the Catholic priesthood in Poland and any of the intelligentsia who were seen as a threat to the Third Reich. In Russia they continued their deadly work with the initial 3,000 Germans being assisted by Ukrainians and Baltic volunteers. Einsatzgruppen 'A' was responsible for the killing of at least 140,000 civilians and added Soviet Political officers to their list of victims. Their brutal behaviour simply pushed thousands of Jews and other potential victims into joining the partisans, who gave them a measure of shelter from the Germans.

German Police forces, the Ordnungspolizei (Order Police) were also active in an anti-partisan role and by 1939 had reached a strength of 131,000 men. Although they did not usually get involved in any front-line fighting, they were involved in executions of partisans in Poland and Russia. They also guarded prison camps, and specific battalions took part in anti-partisan operations – but usually in a support role.

By March 1943 it was estimated that the German Army had a shortfall of 470,000 men at the front and high ranking Wehrmacht officers were looking to expand the use of Russian volunteers. By June 1943 the total number of Hilfswillige was estimated at 320,000, with up to 30 per cent of them being used in combat against the partisans. Reports said that many German units had at least 20 per cent of their front-line strength, made up of Hiwis. German officers reported that they usually fought well and most of the Hiwis had a genuine hatred of the Soviet regime. Even as the war turned against the Germans from late 1942 there were still a large number of Russians, Ukrainians and other nationalities willing to fight for them.

Militia units were also set up in Belorussia and Ukraine to act as support troops for the Germans. In Ukraine they were known as 'Popular Self Defence Corps' (UNS), with a total strength of 180,000 men. Belorussian Militia were known as 'Self Defence Corps' (BNS), which was later changed to 'Security Corps' (BKS) and six battalions were raised. In the summer of 1942 Himmler appointed his adjutant, SS-Gruppenführer Knoblauch as

Chief of the Reichsfürhrer SS Command Staff. He had special responsibility for countering the growing threat of the Soviet partisans. The German Army had nine security divisions, each with six to seven battalions of poorly armed older soldiers. These soldiers were largely unfit for service on the front line, and the divisions were not adequate enough to control and police the territory they were earmarked to garrison.

The main untapped source of anti-partisan forces were in fact the Russian – land owning – peasantry themselves. These hated *kulaks* had been persecuted as class enemies by the Bolsheviks and many thousands were killed or sent to the gulags. Those that were allowed to remain on the land were forced into joining collective farms in the 1930s against their will. If the occupying authorities had returned the farms to the peasants then many would have been prepared to fight to defend them against the partisans. When some peasants asked the Germans for rifles to defend themselves against the partisans and their requisition squads they were turned down. Some small scale experiments were trialled and although the results were favourable the Germans simply did not trust the peasants enough to expand the programme.

It soon became apparent to the Germans that they were going to struggle to fight partisans all over occupied Russia. They began to demand that the other Axis armies in Russia in 1941 police their own rear areas. With an estimated shortfall of 600,000 troops the German Army had already had to stop guarding some of the smaller targets for partisan attacks. Bridges and railway lines that were not on the main communication routes were coming under increasing attacks by the partisans, who saw that they were no longer protected. It would now be up to the Romanian, Hungarian, Italian, Slovakian and Finnish forces to deal with their 'local' partisan problems.

The Romanian Army invaded the Soviet Union in June 1941 and was left in control of the Transnistria region in modern Ukraine, including the port of Odessa. Odessa was taken in August 1941 and the Romanians were at first seen by the population as liberators from the Soviet forces. This honeymoon period was short-lived as a series of massacres against the local population in revenge for heavy losses suffered during the fighting began. In October 1941 the Romanian Army HQ in the port was blown up by local saboteurs killing sixty-one officers, including the highest ranking officer, General Ioan Glogojanu. It was reported that 30,000 Communists and Jews were killed in retaliation for the 'terrorist' attack. Partisan activity soon began throughout Transnistria with pro-Soviet groups and autonomous groups both fighting the Romanians. Partisan activity by the pro-Soviet and anti-Communist groups was concentrated in the north of the region. This was because it was the only region which had dense enough forests for the partisans to shelter in. To deal with the partisan threat three Romanian security divisions, 1st, 2nd and 3rd, were sent into the region. These divisions were made up of one to three regiments, each with three lightly armed Gendarme battalions and a single weak reconnaissance battalion. Each division also had one 75mm artillery battalion armed with First World War era French M1897 field guns. In 1943 a new 24th Infantry Division was formed to perform security duties against the increasing partisan threat. When the Romanian Army was virtually destroyed at Stalingrad its forces came under suspicion from the Germans who took over the region in March 1944.

When the Germans demanded more assistance from their Allies in dealing with the partisan threat, the Hungarians already had troops earmarked for the task. In 1941 the Hungarians had raised five small Security Divisions: 102nd, 105th, 108th, 121st and 124th. These were not intended to serve at the front line and did not have the heavy equipment of a regular unit. Their main role was protecting the supply lines from partisan attack and trying to keep the lines of communication open. The Slovakian forces in Russia had their own anti-partisan formation, the 8,000 strong 'Slovakian Security Division'. Formed on 1 September 1941 the division was responsible for combating partisans operating in areas of northern Ukraine and Belorussia. In addition to infantry the division had a homemade armoured train and field guns and its own air arm in the form of both a fighter and an observation squadron. The fighter squadron had twelve Avia B-534s, while the observation squadron had six Letov S-328s. Armoured vehicles were added to the division's strength during 1942 with six OA vz.30 armoured cars and then a Company of LT-40 light tanks and a number of obsolete vs.33 tankettes, which had never been regarded as capable of front-line service. At the end of the year a unit of six more useful LT-38 medium tanks were added to the armoured units of the division. In May 1943 the division, whose equipment was worn out and not replaced, was sent to fight partisans in far-off Italy and was renamed the 2nd; they were not trusted by their German allies. By January 1944 the division still had 4,500 men but was being kept out of any combat situations, even though in May another 847 men were sent to it as reinforcements.

The Finns fought their own anti-partisan campaign in East Karelia, the territory given up by Finland in return for peace in March 1940. When the Germans invaded the Soviet Union, Finland fought its own campaign to liberate the parts of the country lost in early 1940. During what the Finns called the 'Continuation War 1941–1944', a number of pro-Soviet partisans crossed the Soviet-Finnish border to attack the invaders and target civilian settlements. About 5,000 of these Soviet partisans were operating in East Karelia, but between 1,500 and 2,300 were operational at any time. Volunteers came from all over the Soviet Union and began to pose a real threat to Finnish security and the army's communications. They attacked Finnish villages and killed several hundred civilians, causing special security units to be formed. The Separate Detachment (SAU) was raised in 1943 under the command of Major H. Helenius and launched long-range patrols behind the Soviet lines to cut the partisans off from their supply lines. During the short period of its existence the detachment fought off forty-five partisan attacks, which caused 181 civilian deaths and forty-five wounded.

This Latvian man is a member of the Schutzmannschaft (Auxiliary Police) which served beside the German occupation forces in the Baltic. Formed by Heinrich Himmler on 25 July 1941, the first volunteers probably wore their pre-1941 uniforms. By the end of 1941 the force had expanded to 45,000 men and during 1942 the rapid expansion saw the force expanded to 300,000 men. Although they served alongside German personnel, the ratio to Baltic volunteers was an estimated 1:10. Their role was to provide security in the occupied territories by fighting the partisans in the Baltic states and Ukraine. These forces were known by a confusing number of titles, Schutzmann Schaften, Selbstschutz, Bürgerwehr, Miliz, Ortsmiliz and Ordnungsdienst. (*Author's Collection*)

(**Above**) A sergeant of the Red Army Cossacks has switched sides and joined one of the early units which were ready to serve the German Army. He is still wearing the pre-1941 uniform with peaked cap, and has a former Red Army PPSH-41 submachine gun hanging from his neck. In the early days of Russian collaboration a simple cloth armband was the only distinguishing feature of the anti-Communist volunteers. (*Author's Collection*)

(**Opposite**) In the early stages of the German invasion of the Soviet Union large numbers of keen volunteers came forward to fight for the invaders. This group armed with a handful of Mosin-Nagant M1891 rifles are being given instruction in handling the DT tank machine gun. Many of these volunteers came from the Baltic states and from the Ukraine where Soviet rule had seen millions killed or imprisoned at Stalin's orders. (*Author's Collection*)

(**Above**) A unit of anti-Communist Militia formed in the Lokot region to aid the Germans in their fight against the partisans. There were many reasons why Russians were willing to join these kind of armed groups, but usually the harsh treatment meted out by the Red Army was paramount. The brutal way that Stalin and his NKVD had dealt with people during the 1920s and 1930s built up resentment that came to the fore when the Germans invaded. (*Author's Collection*)

(**Opposite, above**) A unit of recently recruited Cossack cavalry are seen showing off their horsemanship in the new German uniforms with M35 steel helmets. They are all armed with ex-Soviet Mosin-Nagant M1891 rifles issued to them by the German unit to which they are attached. Captured Cossacks were usually given preferential treatment by the German Army, giving the opportunity to fight for them. Cossacks were favoured by the Germans as they claimed ancestry going back to the Ostrogoths of the late Roman period and were not regarded as Slavs. (*Author's Collection*)

(**Opposite, below**) This *sotnia* of anti-Communist Cossacks is seen on patrol on the look out for any signs of partisan activity. In 1941 local German commanders had accepted the assistance of small numbers of Cossacks. When they had proved their reliability and shown their genuine hatred for the Soviet Union more substantial units were raised. Many *sotnias* were raised in Southern Russian regions like the Don and Kuban, where Cossacks had fought for the White Armies during the 1917–1922 Civil War. (*Author's Collection*)

(**Above**) The standard bearer of a newly raised *sotnia* of Don Cossacks from southern Russia displays the usual tricolour flag with a black swastika in the centre in 1943. Don Cossacks had suffered under the rule of the Soviet Union having fought against the Red Army in the 1918 Civil War. Cossacks like these had scores to settle and thought that the Germans could be their salvation in the long struggle against Soviet rule. (*Janucz Piekalkiewicz Collection*)

(**Opposite, above**) The senior officers or *starshina* of a new Don Cossacks squadron gather in the square of a town to discuss their next patrol. These men in their 50s and 60s would have fought for the Whites in the Civil War and some may well have served alongside the Germans in 1918. In that year the German Army invaded Ukraine and Southern Russia under the terms of the Treaty of Brest-Litovsk with the Bolshevik regime. Local Cossacks under the leadership of Ataman Kaledin looked to the Germans to help them in the fight for an independent Don Republic. (*Janucz Piekalkiewicz Collection*)

The personal guard of the German Commander-in-Chief of the 15th Cossack Cavalry Corps stand outside their barracks in their special uniforms with gold chevrons. They are guarding their commander, Major-General Von Pannwitz, a German officer who was proud to command the Cossacks. His men were loyal to him throughout the war and he was to return the compliment by sharing the dire fate of his men when they were sent back to the Soviet Union in 1945. (*Author's Collection*)

(**Above**) These two young Ukrainians belong to one of the seventy-one Ukrainian Schuma battalions who served alongside German forces in the occupied Soviet Union. The Germans were surprised by the welcome they received in Ukraine in the summer of 1941. In reality, and unsurprisingly, the Ukrainians saw the Germans as liberators from several decades of brutal control by the Russians. These two smartly dressed volunteers have been armed with ex-Soviet Mosin-Nagant M1891 rifle and DP-27 light machine gun. The role of men like these in the liquidation of Russian Jews came from a deep-seated hatred of the Jewish people by many Ukrainians which had gone back centuries. (*Author's Collection*)

(**Opposite**) This volunteer of the Osttruppen stands guard over a group of German officers with his PPSH-41 submachine gun. Many of these Eastern volunteers earned the trust of the Germans and their fate was now in the hands of the German Army. It was usually on a local basis that willing Russians were recruited, and most were employed as guards or for convoy protection in the early days of the war. (*Author's Collection*)

(**Opposite**) These Terek Cossacks from the Caucasus are part of a German security unit combating the Red Army in 1942. Terek Cossacks made up the 2nd Brigade of the 1st Cossack Division raised by the Germans. When the Germans retreated from the Caucasus after the defeat of the 6th Army at Stalingrad, some Tereks retreated with them. When the Red Army entered the region in 1943 those who had supported the Germans suffered the wrath of the victors. (*Author's Collection*)

These men belong to the 'Russian National Liberation Army' (RONA), which had begun life as a local anti-Soviet force under the command of former Soviet officer, Bronislaw Kaminski. Kaminski took over from the previous commander who had died in action and expanded RONA into a five regiment strong army with twenty-four captured T-34 medium tanks. This force operated against partisans in the region to the south of the city of Bryansk until the Germans were defeated in fighting for Orel and at the Battle of Kursk. In the summer of 1943 Kaminski led 50,000 men, women and children away from the safety of his fiefdom to follow the retreating German Army. In May 1944 the Germans, desperate for troops, promoted Kaminski to SS-Oberfürhrer and renamed the RONA, 29th SS Division Rona. The RONA had already earned a reputation for cruelty in their 'no holds barred' fighting with the partisans and they were to go on to earn a similar reputation in Warsaw in 1944. (*Author's Collection*)

This Asiatic horseman belongs to the Kalmuck Corps, an exotic formation raised from nomadic Buddhists of Mongol ancestry. These people had settled in an area north-west of the Caspian Sea and west of the River Volga, and like other ethnic peoples were swallowed up by the Soviet Union. When the Germans invaded the region, Kalmucks volunteered to serve as Hiwi volunteers and were eventually allowed to form their own cavalry units. At first they were just a few hundred Kalmucks, but by July 1944 when they had been forced to flee their homeland, there were two brigades with two regiments each, comprising a total of 3,438 officers and men. (*Janucz Piekalkiewicz Collection*)

These three Cossacks are reported to belong to the Kalmuck (Kalmyk Corps) but they may have been recruited from the Russian population of the region. In August 1941 the first Kalmuck formation was formed to help protect the German 6th Army from partisan attacks. Armed with German and captured Soviet weapons, the Kalmucks were forced to retreat with the German Army to the west as they fell back towards Germany. In January 1945 the Kalmucks were largely wiped out in a battle at Radom in Poland, with the survivors being sent to Croatia to fight partisans there. (*Author's Collection*)

A unit of Tartar self defence troops are put through their paces by a German military instructor in 1942. These volunteers are well dressed, with full German Army uniform including M35 steel helmets. Like most Russian and minority units these men have all been issued with the Mosin-Nagant M1891 rifles. Armbands worn by these men show in black German text on a white background, 'Im Dienst der Deutschen Wehrmacht'. (NAC)

These men are volunteers of a Crimean Tartar self defence company, combating the partisans of Crimea in 1942. With a German field-grey great coat and M1934 side cap, the man in the centre has the armband which denotes his role as a willing volunteer for the Wehrmacht. Many of these troops were armed with ex-Red Army Mosin-Nagant M1891 rifles, but this man has a Mauser 98k. (Author's Collection)

On 15 November 1941 the German High Command allowed the recruitment of anti-Communist Turkmenian volunteers to serve in the army. By 30 December it had been decided to raise four legions of Central Asian volunteers coming from a variety of races. These included Turkmenians, Uzbeks, Kirghizs, Kazakhs, Tadziks and Karakalpaks, as well as other lesser known peoples from the region. In August 1943 a Turkestan division was formed and was sent to perform anti-partisan operations in Yugoslavia. These men are wearing German Army uniforms with the armband with a mosque device in the centre and are armed with ex-Soviet Mosin-Nagant M1891 rifles. (*Author's Collection*)

The Slovakian contingent of the Axis forces in Russia from 1941 was the 50,000-strong Mobile Brigade. Like other Axis formations in the Soviet Union, the Slovaks had to contend with partisans in northern Ukraine and Belorussia. A security division was raised to take part in anti-partisan operations, with its own air cover in the form of a fighter squadron and a reconnaissance squadron. In late June 1942 a small company unit of armoured cars was added to the security division's strength and this OA Vz 30 armoured car is part of that force. (*Author's Collection*)

The 62,000-strong Italian Expeditionary Corps in Russia – Corpo di Spedizione Italiano in Russia (CSIR) – served on the Russian Front from July 1941. It was subordinated to the German 11th Army in its early period on the Russian Front and saw widespread action in the autumn of 1941. During the winter of 1941–42 the CSIR began to receive requests, then demands, from the Germans to help in their struggling anti-partisan campaign. Here an Italian interrogates a suspected partisan who is probably just a displaced soldier from the front. (*Author's Collection*)

This Italian 'Black Shirt' is about to go on an anti-partisan operation during the autumn of 1941. In July 1942 the CSIR was reinforced by the Italians and became the 235,000 strong 'Italian Army in Russia' (ARMIR) otherwise known as the 8th Army. One Italian division, the 156th 'Vicenza' Infantry Division, was utilised mainly behind the front line. Its role was protecting lines of communication and performing security duties including anti-partisan operations. Elite Black Shirt 'M' battalions were some of the best units in Russia and could be usually relied on to prosecute their campaign against 'Communists' vigorously. (*Author's Collection*)

(**Above**) Romanian cavalry of the 9th Rosiori Regiment are seen during fighting in the Caucasus in the summer of 1942. As with all of Germany's allies on the Eastern Front, the Romanians were 'requested' to aid the German Army in its ever worsening struggle with the partisans. Cavalry like these were often given the task of keeping a check on the movements of partisan bands in the Romanian Army's rear. (*Author's Collection*)

(**Left**) This Romanian soldier belongs to one of the two security divisions which were given the responsibility of garrisoning the newly won territory of Transnistria. The 1st and 3rd Security Divisions both had a full strength infantry regiment with three battalions. They also had three poorly armed and equipped gendarme battalions, a poorly staffed reconnaissance battalion and a battery of old 75mm field guns. This soldier wears the standard peaked cap with the out-of-date M1930 uniform and is armed with a Mannlicher M1893 rifle. (*Author's Collection*)

A unit of Hungarian Security troops are operating in the rear area of the Stalingrad Front in 1942. They are protecting their lines of communication which were coming under attack by Soviet partisans. The Hungarian Army was given responsibility for the control of large parts of Ukraine and more and more troops were required for this role in 1941–42. (*NAC*)

Three Hungarian Security troops of one of the five light divisions pose with a German Army officer during an anti-partisan operation. As well as infantry the Hungarians used their famous Honvéd cavalry in the security role and these were particularly useful in the wide open steppes of Ukraine. Two of the Hungarians are wearing distinctive insignia on their caps and collars, which probably show that they are security troops rather than front-line soldiers. (*NAC*)

A Hungarian Army machine gunner is taking part in an anti-partisan operation in the rear of their lines in 1942. Up until the end of 1942 and the disastrous defeat at Stalingrad the Hungarians were expected to provide regular infantry units to assist the Germans with hunting down partisans. This man is armed with a German MG30 light machine gun which was adopted by the Hungarians as the Solothurn 31.M Golyószóró. It had been rejected by the Wehrmacht but was adopted by the Austrian Army pre-1938, as well as the Swiss. Three thousand were purchased by Hungary and it remained the main light machine gun in their service until 1945, with 9,000 being produced there. (*Author's Collection*)

General Andrei Vlassov watches one of his men taking part in machine gun practice with his DP-27 light machine gun. When Vlassov a high-ranking and respected Red Army officer had been captured in late 1942 he had proposed raising an anti-Soviet Russian Army from among POWs. He was ignored until Germany was desperate, and then was allowed to gather a number of disparate Russian volunteers into one cohesive force. The so-called Russian Army of Liberation was never a united force, but on paper was formidable, with 125,000 men by 1945. (*Author's Collection*)

An elderly South Caucasian man has been
recruited into a local volunteer unit willing
to fight for the German Army. He is wearing
a white linen armband with the black
lettering in German which denotes his role
within the army. Although he is wearing his
own jacket he should be issued with some
version of the German Army uniform in due
course and has already been given a Mosin-
Nagant M1891 rifle. (*Author's Collection*)

These Cossacks belong to the small Italian
raised unit, the 1st Cossack Volunteer
Sotnia which was formed by the 8th Army
in Russia. This experiment by the Italians
to try to copy the Cossack detachments
raised by the Germans began on 1 April
1943. The unit had one colonel, four officers
and 360 Cossacks, and was attached to the
Italian Army 'Lancers of Novaria' cavalry
regiment. This unit, which was used for
scouting and anti-partisan duties, was
dissolved when the Italians left the war
and most of its personnel chose to join the
German Army. (*Author's Collection*)

Finnish Private Eino Porttimaa belonged to a long-distance scouting unit of the Finnish Army in 1943 and poses with his Suomi KP/-31 submachine gun over his shoulder. These units were tasked with protecting Finnish villages from Soviet partisan attacks in the Savukosi region. (*Sa-kuva 31872679427*)

Finnish men, including soldiers and civilians, collect some Italian Fucile Corto Modello 1891–38 short rifles with which to defend their farms and villages from Soviet partisans in East Karelia. The partisans operated in the region which had been annexed by the Soviet Union after the winter war of 1939–40. Most of their attacks against the Finns were aimed at the civilian population, with only small Finnish units available to defend them. (*Author's Collection*)

Chapter Six

The Warsaw Risings 1943-1944

By 1943 the Polish capital Warsaw had endured a brutal three-and-a-half-year occupation, which saw the population executed for the slightest sign of defiance to the German occupation. Any resistance to the occupation was met with mass executions of hostages and the public hanging of any captured resistance fighters. Although the Polish population suffered terribly, the Jewish population of the city were in a much worse situation. With little to lose, the Polish and the Jewish population in Warsaw were ready to strike back at the vicious regime. It was to be the Jewish people in the ghetto who were to rise up first in what was a hopeless but valiant attempt to gain some revenge on the Germans.

The first rising in Warsaw was confined to the Warsaw Ghetto, where the entire Jewish population of the city and surrounding areas had been forcibly moved in October 1940. After cramming 460,000 Jews into an area of only 1.3 square miles, with every available space filled with families, often over nine to a room, the people were soon desperate. Things only got worse as the population barely survived on starvation rations supplemented by what they could buy on the black market. When the Nazis decided that the slow death of thousands of Jews in ghettos all over Poland was not enough, the 'final solution' was decided upon. In the summer of 1942 mass deportations to 'work camps' from the ghetto began with the population being under few illusions as to the true fate of deportees. A total of 254,000 residents of the ghetto were transported to Treblinka extermination camp, and the vast majority were sent to the gas chambers. In January 1943 it was decided to finish off the remaining 60–70,000 Jews still in the ghetto. However, some of the surviving Jews were determined not to go to their fate without a fight and had organised an uprising to disrupt the deportation. The Jewish fighters were poorly armed with a small numbers of handguns, rifles and homemade weapons smuggled into the ghetto. There were two rival resistance groups, the left-wing 'Jewish Combat Organisation' (ZOB), and the right-wing 'Jewish Military Union' (ZZW), both with about 400 fighters. The ZZW was given a few weapons by the Polish Home Army (AK), which were only a fraction of what was needed to put up a prolonged resistance to the Germans. These included two heavy machine guns, four light machine guns, twenty-one submachine guns, thirty rifles, fifty pistols and 400 grenades.

The ZZW leader, 23-year-old Mordechai Anielwicz, and his fellow fighters were under no illusions about their eventual fate. With nothing to lose they were prepared to sell their lives as dearly as they could, killing as many Germans as they could in the process. Orders to destroy the remains of the ghetto were issued in February, but it took until mid-April for the Germans to organise their forces. The German commander, SS Brigadeführer Jurgen Stroop had only 2,000 troops, and half were largely untrained second-line policemen. Stroop had been supplied with some artillery pieces and got air support from the nearby Luftwaffe units. When the assault on the ghetto began on 19 April, the Jewish fighters had only a small store of ammunition for their various pistols and rifles. They did manage to capture some weapons from the Germans they killed, but were soon forced to withdraw into the sewers. A step by step advance into the ghetto saw surprise attacks by the Jewish fighters met with attempts by the Germans to drown them or gas them out of the sewers. As the Germans advanced they totally demolished the buildings giving little shelter for the defenders. On 8 May, Mordechai Anielwicz and his command were surrounded at their HQ Bunker in Ulica Mila 18 and died fighting. Within a week the resistance had virtually ended and Stroop could claim to have killed at least 1,000 Jewish fighters. At least 5,000 Jews had died in the firestorms created by the Germans and the total casualty rate of the Jewish population was 56,000. Any Jews who surrendered were either immediately shot or sent to their delayed fate in Treblinka, having had at least the satisfaction of killing about 300 Germans. The Germans claimed that they only lost seventeen dead and ninety-three wounded, but the sheer ferocity of the fighting suggests that their estimates are too low. After the end of the uprising the only surviving ZOB Commander, Marek Edelman, said that the Jews' inspiration to fight was: 'Not to allow the Germans alone to pick the time and place of our deaths.'

In the early summer of 1944 the Red Army was advancing through Eastern Poland and were drawing close to the Polish capital, Warsaw. The Home Army (Armia Krajowa) was now prepared to rise up in the capital and seize it, or at least take strategic sections of the city.

They hoped that once they had taken the city they could welcome the Red Army and thereby gain some influence in their 'liberated' country. Unknown to the AK the Red Army had no intention of coming to the rescue of an uprising, but would let the two sides battle it out to the finish. They would sit tight on the outskirts of Warsaw and then deal with whoever came out on top when the fighting ended. In late July rumours of an all out Red Army attack on Warsaw made the AK more likely to begin its uprising. On the morning of 1 August orders went out from the AK leadership to begin the long-awaited uprising. Ammunition was in short supply as much of the AK's limited stocks had been sent into the countryside to help the fighting there. The Home Army divided its forces into eight city districts with a total of 600 companies moving across the city to their designated objectives from 17.00 hours. In the early hours of the rising some of the AK objectives were taken with a number of German troops killed, along with a number of civilians killed in the crossfire. AK losses mounted in the first twenty-four hours rose to 2,500, with most lost in assaults on heavily defended German positions. Rifles, pistols and a few machine guns were the main weapons of the AK, along with plenty of Molotov cocktails. The uprising was to be dealt with by 17,000 German and foreign troops under the command of SS-Obergruppenführer Erich von dem Bach-Zelewski. Foreign volunteers were made up of Azerbaijanis, Cossacks and Russians of the SS RONA Brigade, and a number of diverse and often unsavoury units. When these troops advanced against the AK barricades and strongholds they killed any civilians who got in their way.

In the western suburbs of Warsaw many thousands of civilians, men, women and children, were killed. The atrocities were eventually limited to the killing of male civilians, with women and children taken to a transit camp outside the city. Fighting intensified and the AK were able to capture a number of tanks and armoured vehicles they had cornered in the city's narrow side streets. As it became apparent to the AK that no Soviet help was going to be received, they begged for help from their government-in-exile in London. A hundred and four tons of Allied arms were dropped to the AK during the uprising and fifty-five tons were parachuted into the city by the Red Air Force. The token supplies from the Red Army were in support of what the Soviets called a 'purely adventuristic affair' that they were not willing 'to lend its hand to'. Included in the British arms were a number of PIAT anti-tank launchers, which were put to good use, and a large number of German small arms, including the latest assault rifles. By the end of August the fighting had turned into a bloody stalemate, with the AK developing a number of new weapons and booby traps to make up for their lack of ammunition. Both sides were exhausted and losses were mounting and the Germans were aware that the Red Army was waiting to move as soon as the uprising ended. September saw an agreed safe removal of 25,000 civilians negotiated by the Germans and the Polish Red Cross. Offers of 'combatant rights' being granted to the AK by the Germans were dismissed by the suspicious Poles. A twenty-four-hour truce in late September allowed 9,000 civilians to be evacuated and some trust was developed by both sides. With AK forces now only holding onto its strongest positions the Polish leadership knew they could not resist for much longer. On 2 October, with only the centre of the city still in Polish hands, the AK leader General Bor-Komorowski agreed to surrender. Although a costly failure, the whole free world admired the bravery of the AK and even the Germans had to give their grudging respect to their enemy. At least 20,000 AK fighters were killed in action but it was the civilian population that suffered the most. Civilian casualties were estimated at 150,000 from execution in the early days of the uprising, and from the indiscriminate German shelling of the city. German losses were reported to be 10,000, which showed how fierce the poorly armed Poles had fought for sixty-three days.

One of the main leaders of the Jewish resistance fighters was Mordechai Anielewicz, seen here in this poor quality photograph. He led the 'Jewish Fighting Organisation' which was the largest armed group involved in the Warsaw Ghetto Rising. Aneilewicz was thrown into a Soviet jail in 1940 and returned to his home city of Warsaw where he began to organise Jews into resistance groups in the ghetto. Reports of mass murder of Jews forced the pace of plans for a rebellion against the German occupiers. After becoming the leader of underground resistance group the ZZW, he led them in a futile but courageous rising and died during fighting for his HQ bunker on 8 May beside his girlfriend and his fellow commanders. (*Author's Collection*)

Two dishevelled resistance fighters surrender to the Germans during the Warsaw Ghetto Uprising. They had been captured on 27 April, nine days into the uprising when most fighters were running out of ammunition. Homemade weapons often had to be relied upon and the capture of German arms was a priority for all of the fighters. The vast majority of captured fighters were either immediately shot or sent to Treblinka extermination camp or one of three labour camps. In the first week in November 1943 all of the captured Jewish fighters were killed over a three-day period. (General Stroop Album)

Three female fighters of the HeHalutz Zionist organisation are pictured just after capture by The Germans. They were accused of throwing Molotov Cocktails and passing on messages between the various fighting groups. The fate of these girls is known, with only the girl on the right, Malka Zdrojewicz, surviving the war. Bluma Wyszogrodka in the centre was shot in the ghetto and Rachela Wyszogrodzka on the left was gassed in Auschwitz. Malka was one of only 34 Fighters to survive emigrating to Israel in 1946. The main role of these female fighters was in throwing Molotov Cocktails at the German attackers at which they became very adept. (General Stroop Album)

SS-Gruppenführer Jurgen Stroop, the commander of forces employed in the crushing of the Warsaw Ghetto Uprising, looks on as his men destroy the remains of the ghetto. Having served on the Eastern Front from 1941, Stroop was given command of the anti-ghetto forces. He was ruthless in the extreme and at the end of the month-long rising his men killed 57,000 of the surviving residents, or sent them to their death in extermination camps. His force included two battalions of Waffen-SS, 100 order police, and about 100 security police. Stroop had 9,000 troops of the 3rd SS Infantry Division held in reserve if they were required. (*Author's Collection*)

SS-Lieutenant-General Erich von dem Bach-Zelewski (1899–1972) spent the Second World War organising various anti-Jewish and anti-partisan operations. During the early weeks of Operation Barbarossa he commanded some of the notorious Einsatzgruppen units as they robbed, brutalised and killed any Jews they could capture. He was in command of these extermination troops when they killed 35,000 Jews in two weeks in Riga, Latvia. Having suffered nightmares and a nervous breakdown he was sent to hospital to 'recover'. When he was recovered he returned to his previous role and organised anti-partisan operations in Belorussia and Northern Russia. During his command of these operations he insisted on the most brutal treatment of partisans and Russian peasants alike. He finished his inglorious military career in command of all the various forces gathered to suppress the Warsaw Uprising between August and October 1944. (*Author's Collection*)

SS-Brigadefürhrer Mizieslaw Kaminski was one of the most infamous characters found on the Eastern Front during the Second World War. He was a Russian and an anti-Communist who helped organise a militia in the Lokotj region in autumn 1941. By 1944 he had 20,000 men under his command, having taken over from the original commander who had been killed in battle. Kaminski's bad behaviour was too much even for his fellow SS commanders and he was arrested and executed during the rising. (*Author's Collection*)

An AK fighter poses with a ZB-30 light machine gun over his shoulder in the early days of the Warsaw Uprising. This weapon was never in service with the Polish Army but may have been captured from the German Army during the pre-rising period. He is wearing civilian dress and has not even been able to acquire an armband or over insignia to show his allegiance. (*Author's Collection*)

A well turned out squad of AK fighters are inspected by their commander at the start of the Warsaw Uprising. The men and boys have assembled their own clothing, with the young boy at the front adding a white-over-red pennant badge to his cap. This unit has been well armed with Mauser rifles which may be Polish Karabinek wz.1929s or captured German 98ks. (*Author's Collection*)

Teenage girl messengers for the AK pose in their uniforms with the red and white ribbons on their peaked caps. They used any possible means to get their messages from one unit to another and their casualty rate must have been terrible. These young women were said by some commanders to be braver than their male comrades under fire. Some were issued with bravery medals during the rising and promoted to corporal as a sign of appreciation by the AK command. (*Author's Collection*)

Men of Oskar Dirlewanger's disreputable SS unit of former poachers, seen emerging from cover in Warsaw, had officially been collected from the prisons of Germany. In reality the majority of these anti-partisan troops had been recruited from concentration camps as well as prisons. The 49-year-old Dirlewanger had a doctorate in political science and had spent time in prison himself for molesting a minor. After being released he was given command of the penal unit of desperate volunteers having used his murky contacts in the SS hierarchy to gain command. His men turned out to be brutal but effective anti-partisan troops, and 2,000 of them were sent to Warsaw to assist in the crushing of the rising. (*Author's Collection*)

(**Above**) Men of Kaminski's RONA brigade fire from their trench during the Warsaw Uprising where they made up a poorly trained force. Most of Kaminski's men at Warsaw were younger recruits who were selected because they had no dependants. When the Germans had retreated from the area controlled by Kaminski's brigade they also fled, totalling 50,000 soldiers and civilian camp followers. At Warsaw they had been given the grand designation, 29th Division, Waffen SS 'Rona' – Russian. They proved to be a totally undisciplined mob and most were found to be poorly trained, although well armed. This group have a MG-42 machine gun, a MP-40 submachine gun and a PPSH-41 submachine gun. (*Author's Collection*)

(**Opposite, above**) AK fighters examine a PIAT anti-tank launcher which has been parachuted into Warsaw in the midst of the uprising. These effective weapons were put into good use during the fighting and managed to destroy or disable a number of German vehicles. The man on the right of the photograph is wearing an M35 steel helmet which has been decorated with the Polish eagle emblem. (*Author's Collection*)

(**Opposite, below**) These AK fighters have acquired a Soviet DP-27 machine gun which was dropped into Warsaw by the Red Air Force. Stalin was reluctant to support the rising and saw the rebels as future obstacles to his takeover of Eastern Poland when the war ended. In total fifty-five tons of supplies were dropped by the Russians and this machine gun is presumably part of the insufficient arms the AK received. (*Author's Collection*)

This well turned out unit of the Home Army AK at the start of the Warsaw Uprising is the company of 2nd Lieutenant Janusz Zapolski, with the nom-de-guerre 'Janusz'. It is part of the 'Harnas Group', which was commanded by Lieutenant Marian Krawczyk, whose pseudonym was 'Harnas'. (*Author's Collection*)

AK fighters defend a barricade in strongly contested Jerozolimskie Avenue, only one man appears to have a rifle. The rest of the fighters appear to be armed only with hand grenades and Molotov cocktails, which could be deadly at close range. Anyone throwing one of these homemade weapons had to have nerves of steel as they usually had to expose themselves to enemy fire. (*Author's Collection*)

A smiling boy AK messenger has a dispatch under his arm and a rifle over his shoulder with a grenade clutched in his hand. As more adult fighters were killed or injured there were more arms to go around the younger volunteers who had previously been unarmed. This boy had also been issued a captured German M35 steel helmet which would have white over red cloth insignia somewhere on it. (*Author's Collection*)

(**Above**) Polish fighters defend a barricade during the early fighting for Warsaw and all wear M35 steel helmets taken from dead German troops. The weaponry carried by the men is also mainly from captured sources, with an MP-40 submachine gun, a P-08 Luger automatic-pistol and a small automatic pistol. (*Author's Collection*)

(**Opposite, above**) This AK unit is the 'Krawiec' Company, raised in the Mokotów district of Warsaw is a well turned out unit. On the left of the photograph is 2nd Lieutenant Stanislaw Milczynski (Gryf), the Company Commander. The Mokotów district of the city was to suffer particularly badly at the hands of the German forces and their foreign auxiliaries. When the district surrendered on 27 September, many of the remaining AK fighters had withdrawn through the sewers. Some unfortunately got lost and came out of the sewers in the middle of a German-held sector, and 140 of them were shot on Dworkowa Street. Another ninety-eight were shot on Chocimska Street and these victims were heavily beaten before their execution. (*Private Collection – Public Domain*)

(**Opposite, below**) A mixed group of Russians fighting for the Germans in Warsaw in 1944 check a street map of the city. They are made up of Cossacks and an armoured crewman of the Kaminski Brigade. This disparate group of Eastern volunteers made up a large part of the forces charged with crushing the rising, with 50 per cent speaking only Russian. Among the 12,000 men who made up the German attack force were Russians, Azeri's, Turkmen and Ukrainians. (*NAC*)

Two AK female fighters take a smoke break and chat to one of their male wounded comrades. They are on Wenecka Street and belong to 'Parasol' Battalion, the insignia of which is on the field cap of the wounded fighter. This unit distinguished itself during the rising and its fighters were well known for their ability to move quickly around the sewers to make attacks on the Germans. (*Bender*)

A Cossack gunner prepares to fire his 37mm PAK 35/36 anti-tank gun towards AK positions during the rising. The Cossacks, who were part of the German forces sent to crush the rising, were not well trained or disciplined. They were made up of the 3rd Cossack Regiment, the 69th, 209th, 572nd Cossack Battalions and 580 Squadron of the Cossack cavalry. During the two-month duration of the rising, the Germans were scratching around to find any unit regardless of its size to join the forces tasked with defeating the AK. (*NAC*)

Among the various German-recruited foreign units taking part in the suppression of the Warsaw Uprising were two Battalions of the 111th Azerbaijani Regiment. Azerbaijani units took part in front-line fighting in the Ukraine, Belarus, Poland and on the Caucasus front. These troops were better regarded than other foreign contingents as they had proved themselves pre-1944 under the command of Abdurrahman Fatalibeyli. These troops are armed mainly with German rifles and machine guns, but one man has acquired a PPSH-41 submachine gun. (*Author's Collection*)

Two AK commanders discuss their plans for the defence of their sector of Warsaw, while two civilian volunteers listen intently. Both men have 'acquired' camouflage anoraks from the Germans or their foreign volunteers, and have added their own insignia to them. One man has sewn a white-over-red flag onto his beret, while the other man has a metal Polish Eagle badge on the front of his cap. Most AK fighters had at least a white-over-red armband to show their allegiance and to stop any problems with friendly fire from their own side. (*Author's Collection*)

(**Above**) This AK fighter is using a 'K' pattern flamethrower, which was produced in occupied Poland by the resistance's munitions producers. About 200 of these weapons were made, but by the outbreak of the rising there were only thirty or so still in AK hands. The flamethrower needed a crew of four to operate it, a commander, a gunner and two men to carry the fuel cans. Despite it being homemade, the 'K' pattern came as a major shock to the Germans when it was used, and some additional ones were made during the rising. (*Author's Collection*)

(**Left**) An AK fighter armed with a recently dropped Sten MK2 submachine and wearing a captured M35 steel helmet sits on a wall for a photograph. These guns were air dropped into Poland by the SOE and some were produced by Home Army engineers in small workshops. The so-called 'Popski' Stens were made under the supervision of Ryszard Bialostocki in Warsaw and marked as 'made in England' to put the Germans off the scent. The main body of the gun was made from hydraulic cylinders produced for hospital equipment. (*Author's Collection*)

(**Above**) AK fighters pose at their post on Stawki Street in the Wola District of Warsaw during the uprising. They have acquired a great deal of uniform items, equipment and weaponry from the enemy, who had been taken by surprise in the early stages of the rising. One man has a Thompson submachine gun, which may have been supplied to the Poles in the 1930s as they developed their own type. A Wz. 39 'Mors' submachine gun had been under development in 1939 and was to be issued to the Polish Army during the early 1940s. (*Author's Collection*)

(**Right**) A boy messenger wearing full uniform is seen with his letter satchel over his shoulder and is wearing a M35 steel helmet. The young women, girls and boys who ran the gauntlet of fire between the lines in the centre of the city had a precarious existence. Getting a message through from one isolated unit to another involved often running past enemy positions swiftly enough to avoid being shot. Warsaw's sewers were used by these messengers but they held their own dangers, including the overwhelming noxious fumes. (*Author's Collection*)

(**Above**) A young Armia Krajowa fighter aims at German positions during the Warsaw Uprising, armed with a Polish produced submachine gun. The Blyskawica – Lightning submachine gun, was produced in secret workshops during 1943 and 1944 to a Polish design. It was modelled partly on the Sten MKII, copies of which were also built by the Poles and an estimated 740 were constructed by AK engineers. (*Author's Collection*)

(**Opposite, above**) A group of well armed AK fighters take advantage of a pause in the fighting to have their photographs taken. They have all acquired firearms, with the young man on the right having a German MP-40, while two of his comrades have Mausers. The other fighter appears to have captured a P08 Luger automatic, probably from the corpse of a dead German officer. Two wear Polish Army Wz. 31 steel helmets, while the other young man has a Polish version of the French Adrian helmet worn by the Polish Cavalry in 1939. (*Author's Collection*)

(**Opposite, below**) Young AK fighters prepare to fire their recently arrived PIAT (British Projector, Infantry Anti-tank) anti-tank launcher against German armour during the rising. The RAF-dropped PIATs were retrieved from their protective containers along with spare projectiles. It was estimated that the AK had seventy of these weapons in the early days of the rising with a total of 250 being dropped into Warsaw by 12 September. (*Author's Collection*)

The commander of the Home Army, General Tadeusz Bor-Komorowski, bows his head as he formally acknowledges the surrender of his forces which took place on 2 October. He shakes hands with SS-Obergruppenführer Bach-Zelewski, the commander of German forces during the Warsaw Uprising. Bor-Komorowski's fate was better than many of his fighters; he was interned in Germany in a prisoner of war camp and survived the war. Despite the insistence of his captors, he refused to order the capitulation of other Home Army units outside Warsaw. (*Author's Collection*)

Chapter Seven

Czechoslovakia 1940-1944

The young nation of Czechoslovakia was the sacrificial lamb that delayed the start of the Second World War by over a year. The Munich Agreement saw the embattled nation pressured and coerced into giving up the Sudetenland, with its large German population, in 1938. This agreement only gave Czechoslovakia a short respite and in early 1939 the remains of the country were invaded by Germany, which divided the nation into four entities in March 1939. The Sudetenland, with its large ethnic German population, had already become part of 'greater' Germany; Southern Slovakia was handed over to Hungary, and what remained of Slovakia became an 'independent' state under the Fascist rule of the right-wing cleric Jozef Tiso. Bohemia and Moravia became a protectorate of Germany with a German-controlled puppet government under former Czech President Emil Hacha. The population of the protectorate soon found out how harsh German rule was going to be, with thousands of men sent to Germany as forced labour. Meanwhile, the well-established Czech war industry was totally exploited to supply armaments to the ever-hungry German military. Poor rations in the protectorate were mirrored in conditions for the Czechs in Germany, causing more resentment. Adolf Hitler was quietly wary of the Czech people, who he judged to be a capable and resourceful people, after spending his early life within the Austro-Hungarian Empire. He may have been lured into thinking that the Czechs would be easily controlled after their government's capitulation to his demands in 1938 and 1939. The Czechs and many Slovaks quietly seethed and waited for a chance to rise against their occupiers.

Resistance in the former Czechoslovakia was, however, slow to become established, as the German authorities quickly clamped down savagely on any signs of dissent. The Czech government-in-exile in London tried to contact what resistance there was in early 1940 and amalgamated the various groups into the 'Central Leadership of Resistance at

Home' – Ustredni Vedeni Odboje Domaciho (UVOD). There were a number of partisan groups under the umbrella of the UVOD, including the 'Political Centre' – Politicke Ustredi (PU). Other groups were the 'We Remain Faithful' group (PVVZ), and the 'Nations Defence' – Obrana Naroda (ON). Communist resistance groups complied with its orders from Moscow not to resist the Germans while their non-aggression agreement with Nazi Germany was in place. When the new German administrator of Bohemia-Moravia, Reinhard Heydrich, arrived in Prague in September 1941 things got even worse for the Czechs. One of his first orders to his men was to crackdown on any resistance; 5,000 resisters were duly arrested and swiftly executed. Only small cells of UVOD personnel survived the purge and they were told by the government-in-exile to take a 'defensive' attitude to the occupiers. In May 1942, against the wishes of the Czechs in London and the UVOD, two Czech SOE agents were parachuted into the country. Their mission was to assassinate Heydrich and this was achieved in early June 1942, with the Nazi leader taking a few days to die. Severe reprisals meted out by the Germans included the complete destruction of the village of Lidice, with every man and woman, and most children, slaughtered.

In the aftermath of the Heydrich assassination and the German reprisals, partisan groups began to form during 1942. Although these were not strong in numbers they did begin to attack the occupiers and particularly the railway system. Any partisan forces which were organised in Bohemia and Moravia struggled to survive as the countryside did not really suit a full time insurgent force. In the east of former Czechoslovakia, the Slovakian mountains and forests provided conditions more suitable to the partisans. The early partisan movement started in the Beskydy Mountains on the border between Slovakia and the protectorate of Bohemia and Moravia. A lack of weaponry stifled the resistance and there were never enough rifles and other small arms to go around. From the middle of 1944 the growing Czech partisan movement began to make more attacks against the German-controlled railway system. By April 1945 the fighting in Moravia had changed dramatically from small-scale widespread acts of sabotage of the railway system, to full-scale partisan warfare.

The largest Czech partisan group was the 'Jan Ziska' Brigade which had its base in the Hostyn-Vsetin Mountains of Southern Moravia. They crossed the border from Slovakia in September 1944 and began to sabotage the transport system of Moravia from their bases there. German police units sent to deal with this new threat were in turn attacked by the partisans and often destroyed. Any attacks on German or puppet forces resulted in strong retaliation by the occupiers, including the mass shooting of hostages. Regardless of these harsh measures, or because of them, the Jan Ziska Brigade continued to flourish and grew to 1,500 fighters, controlling large parts of Moravia when the war ended in April 1945.

Another partisan Group was the 'Josef Hyblf-Brodescky' Brigade of the Vasclavik Division, which operated from late 1944 in the Orlicke Mountains of Northern Bohemia. In May 1945 the Brigade had 5,000 men who were armed with a single 75mm field gun and an improvised armoured train called 'Spark of Freedom'. The brigade had a number of motor vehicles with twenty motorcycles, twenty cars and sixty trucks to move the partisans around. Partisan groups in Bohemia and Moravia had grown to 120 by the spring of 1945, with a total of 7,500 fighters. Czech partisans were highly successful in disrupting the German and Slovakian war effort by sabotaging railways and damaging roads and bridges, especially in the mountainous regions. However, the number of active partisans in Bohemia and Moravia was limited by the lack of armaments. Some arms did arrive via the Red Army in the closing stages of the war although the Soviets were reluctant to support a non-Communist group.

The first partisans in Slovakia had been formed in March 1942, comprising factory workers and deserters from the Slovakian Army. During German retreats in front of the Red Army there were a number of Czechs who volunteered to join their ranks. Slovak partisans were said to number between 18,000 and 26,000 men and women, with some of the larger groups having up to 7,000 fighters. In the Lower Tatra region there was reported to be 7,000 partisans of the Lieutenant-Colonel Sukajev Group. Other larger groups were the 3,600 fighters under the command of Major Jegorov in Central Slovakia, and 2,500 partisans of Group Capajev in Eastern Slovakia, which was named after the Russian Civil War hero Chapaev. Two other larger units were the 2,400 fighters of the Group 1st Lieutenant Velicko in the Turiec region, and the 1,700 men of Group Captain Bielik in Central Slovakia. Group Captain Valjansky had 1,600 fighters and also operated also in the centre of the country. The other 11 Groups numbered from the 1,300 men of Group Lieutenant Secansky in Western Slovakia, to the 120 men under Major Jaromov, whose partisans operated at times throughout the country.

Slovakian partisan leader Villian Zingor was a Slovakian Army reserve officer, but when called to front-line service on the Eastern Front in July 1943 he refused to go and took to the hills. By spring 1944 he had managed to pull together a 1,300 strong partisan force made up of fellow deserting soldiers, men who had escaped from German prison camps and patriotic volunteers. Included in his ranks were at least 300 Jews, who were accepted into the partisan force despite the antisemitism of much of the

Slovak population. Jews usually had to hide their faith from some of their comrades, at least until they had proved themselves as good fighters. Zingor soon had enough men to form a viable partisan force which operated around the town of Bystricka. For a few months his partisans, armed largely with ex-Slovakian small arms and some war-booty German weapons, were content to defend their mountain bases. In late August Zingor decided to merge his forces with those of another local partisan leader, Piotr Velicek, whose forces operated around Sklabin. The united partisan force was titled the 'General Milan Rastilov Stefanik 2nd Brigade', and Villian Zingor took command. The Brigade operated in the Rajecka Valley and managed to defend the mountains around their bases ready to move against the Slovakian puppet government of Tiso. In October 1944 the brigade moved to support the Slovak Uprising in the vicinity of Martinské Hole and were part of the 18,000 partisans supporting the rebellion. One distinct Jewish partisan group was the 'Novaky Brigade', formed from inmates of the concentration camp by the same name in Slovakia. In late August 1944 the Jewish prisoners overthrew the guards of the camps and called for able-bodied men to join them in fighting the Germans; 250 agreed, and with the help of friendly anti-German locals were able to get enough arms to join the Slovak Uprising the next day. (see below)

The main opposition to the German occupation of Bohemia Moravia and the pro-German regime in Slovakia were the two uprisings in 1944 and 1945. In 1943 the opposition to the pro-German Slovak regime of Tiso and its support of the Axis powers began to grow. After the German defeat at Stalingrad, desertions from the Slovakian Armed Forces grew and dissent in the ranks also spread. Future partisan groups began to organise and formed the 'Slovak National Council', which contacted the Czech government-in-exile in London. By mid-1944 the council were ready to launch a revolution against the Fascist government of Tiso. The catalyst for the rebellion came when a fighting group was raised in the Novaky concentration camp. This rebellion saw the formation of the 'Novaky Partisan Brigade', which took over the camp on 28 August. As with Italy, the Germans decided to invade their client state on the 28th to crush any chance of a change of sides by the Slovaks. At the same time, Slovak Army General Jan Golian gave the order to start a general insurrection and 18,000 Slovaks rose up to fight the German troops stationed in Slovakia on the 29th. By September there were about 60,000 Slovakian fighters battling with the Germans and their Slovak Fascist allies. The rebels took the city of Banska Bystrica in Central Slovakia, declaring it their capital, and had control of about 60 per cent of the country. They established a radio station and began printing their own newspapers and set up local assemblies.

While the rebels in Central Slovakia were strengthening their control they were less successful in the East of the country, where the attempts of the rebels failed dismally. A 40,000 strong German and Slovakian Fascist force defeated a rebel army in the East and forced them to surrender. Rebel forces in the East had the best troops and equipment and their defeat knocked the stuffing out of their cause. The Slovakian rebels had planned to send their Eastern army to attack the German Army from the rear. Now their only plan was to hold their remaining positions until the advancing Soviet Red Army could rescue their forces. Rebel forces had been able to capture a number of Slovakian government-held airfields but did not have the ammunition for the German planes they captured. Instead, they had to use several obsolete types of biplane aircraft of the Slovakian Air Force. During the uprising these out-of-date planes were able, alongside anti-aircraft guns, to shoot down an impressive total of forty Luftwaffe aircraft.

Despite some setbacks the Germans were unwilling to give in to the rebels and moved reinforcements in from nearby occupied territories. They were able to double their available forces in mid-October and soon crushed the uprising, capturing a large number of rebels. By the end of October the rebels were virtually defeated; their capital at Banska Bystrica fell on the 27th. Rebel forces withdrew to nearby Donovaly, but the remaining fighters were well and truly demoralised. The joint rebel leaders Golian and Viest ordered their men to go to the hills to continue the resistance as guerrillas. Both rebel leaders fell into German hands and were taken back to Germany where they were executed at the end of the war. With only limited support initially, the uprising was almost certain to fail; support from the Soviet Union totalled 350 rifles and 150 anti-tank rifles. They did receive the support of some Soviet fighters from the 1st Czechoslovak Fighter Aviation Regiment whose Lavochkin planes were flown by Czechs and led by Stanislav Rejthar.

Despite their pleas they were delayed in supporting the uprising by their Soviet superiors and only took part from 17 September, three weeks after the uprising began. After landing in Slovakia the pilots flew bombing and strafing missions against the Germans and the Hlinka Guard, but soon ran out of fuel and ammunition. The rebels did also have the support of three armoured trains formerly of the Slovakian Army: the 'Stefanik', the 'Hurban' and the 'T.G. Mararyk'. Rebel forces were eventually faced by 48,000 tough and battle-hardened German troops supported by local Slovak Fascist forces. Most of the Slovak Fascists were from the Hlinka Guard a uniformed militia which supported the Tiso regime. They were given weapons and training by the Germans and fought desperately to defeat the uprising.

Ex-Hlinka Guardsmen were organised into 'Emergency Divisions' or 'Flying Squads', known as 'POHG', with a total of 5,867 volunteers coming forward. These divisions were also known as 'rapid' units of both the Hlinka Guard and the Hlinka Youth Volunteers. The Hlinka Guard were also formed into field companies which fought fanatically against the rebels. The uprising had initial success as they faced only 9,000 Germans, but their forces expanded with first 3,900 arriving to join them and another 2,000 following shortly after. In addition, the 14th Waffen-Grenadier Division of the SS arrived, giving the German commander SS-Obergruppenführer Gottlob Berger a substantial force. When the Germans defeated the Eastern Slovak Army, which was the best rebel force, the morale of the insurgents was severely affected; 25,000 Slovak troops were disarmed and interned, and any that escaped capture usually joined the Slovak partisans. Other Slovak formations in the West did not join the rising as expected and the Red Army changed its plans to invade Slovakia to support the rising. With no outside support for the uprising forthcoming, the rebels established a defensive line which was soon pierced by the Germans.

It still took until mid-October for the growing German and Tiso forces to finally defeat the uprising. All of the rebels' armoured forces had been destroyed by the Germans and although they still had 36,000 men, the leaders of the uprising knew that defeat was inevitable. German reinforcements included the notorious SS Brigade Dirlewanger and 18th Panzer Grenadier Division of the SS, allowing the Germans to encircle the rebel-held area. The final offensive began on 18 October and by the 28th the leaders of the rising issued orders for their men to cease fighting and to join the partisans in the mountains. Victorious German and Tiso forces took their revenge even while the days of the Slovak regime were numbered. The Jewish population was now persecuted as the Tiso regime cooperated in the execution or deportation of 14,000. Another 30,000 Slovaks were deported to Germany, ending up as slave labourers, while some also ended up in concentration camps. Any rebels who fell into their hands, and the Jewish population, were either executed or sent to concentration camps. Official figures for the number of Slovak insurgents killed was 3,000, although the true figures must have been much higher, with 10,000 captured and 1,000 dying in prison.

By early 1945 the Germans were fast losing control of Czechoslovakia as the Red Army advanced close to the capital at Prague. In an effort to stop the spread of partisan activity, especially against the vital railways, everyone willing to fight them was armed. The pro-German forces included scattered units of the Waffen SS, security police and ethnic-German Volkssturm. During March and April, despite their best efforts, the Axis forces were losing control of the railways.

From 6 May until the 11th the Red Army, with 1,770,700 Russians, 139,500 Romanians, 69,500 Poles and 48,400 Czechs, enveloped Prague. Defending the city were 650,000 men of the German Army Group Centre and 430,000 men of the Army Group Ostmark, as well as almost 10,000 Hungarians. The day before the launch of the offensive on 5 May 1945, Czech Police had burst into the Prague radio station and began fighting with the SS guards in the building. In support of this uprising an estimated 30,000 civilians took to the streets and began to build barricades across the city centre roads. According to varying reports they constructed between 1,600 to 2,000 barricades and waited for the expected attack by German and pro-German Czechs. These troops included units of the Waffen SS, who had been withdrawn from the hard-pressed front line to deal with the rebels.

The US 3rd Army under the command of General George S. Patton had entered Czechoslovakia but were forbidden from going to the aid of Prague. The Soviet leader Joseph Stalin had asked the Americans to allow his troops to liberate the city and they were worried about the Red Army's attitude to any US move on Prague. Meanwhile, fighting in the city had begun in earnest on the 7th, while the city's population started a series of acts of defiance on the streets. The uprising took a surprising turn when the rebels were able to persuade anti-Soviet Russian soldiers of the 1st Division of the ROA (Russian Liberation Army) to come to their aid. These 'turncoat' Russians had been formed into two Divisions in January 1945 under the overall command of ex-Soviet general, Andrey Vlasov. The 20,000 strong 1st Division were camped near Prague in May 1945 and their commander, Major General Bunyachenko, decided to intervene on the Czechs' side. He wanted to curry favour with the Allies and hoped that by fighting for the rebels he would save his men from their expected fate when the Nazis fell.

The ROA units were reluctantly welcomed by the rebels when they arrived in Prague on the 6th and were able to counter an offensive against the Czechs by Waffen SS units. The ROA had been well supplied with artillery and other heavy weaponry which halted the SS attack. Meanwhile, the Germans sent a pair of Me 262 jet fighters to attack the centre of Prague, while the rebels had found a large number of rifles and hundreds of Panzerfaust anti-tank launchers in German stores. They also captured five light tanks, which were put on parade in the centre of the city as their armament had been removed. During the few days of the rising there were a number of atrocities committed by both sides, but the fighting quickly turned into a stalemate. By the 7th the fighting had largely died down and many Germans were looking to escape westwards to surrender to the US 3rd Army. The ROA also tried to surrender to the US forces but opposition by the Czech Communists meant they would eventually be handed over to the Soviet authorities. The Soviet Red Army's 'Prague Strategic Offensive' of 6–11 May saw the Czech capital liberated in one of the last actions of the Second World War.

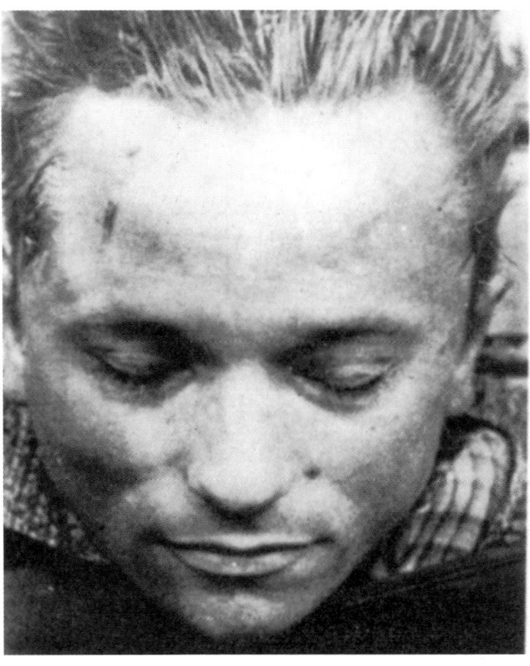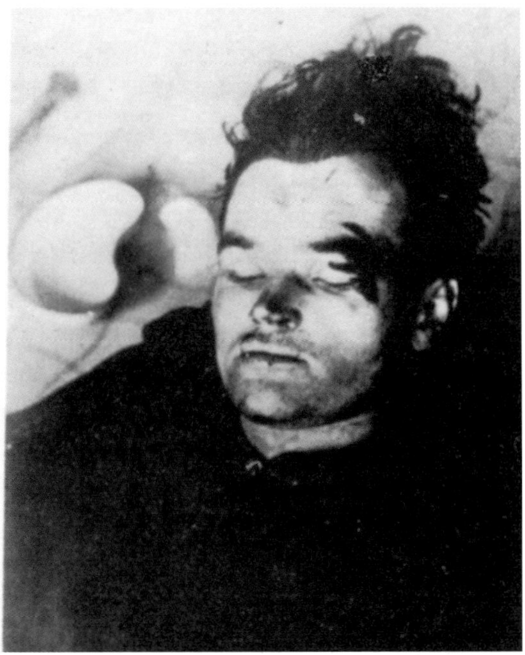

The British SOE (Special Operations Executive) began dropping Czech agents into the country from 1941, and in May 1942 two were ordered to assassinate Reinhard Heydrich, the Nazi 'protector' of Bohemia-Moravia. This assassination was ordered by the Czech government-in-exile and was opposed by the Czech resistance. The two dead assassins, Josef Gabcik and Jan Kubis, have been photographed after they were cornered by the Germans in the crypt of a Prague church. Besides the two agents many Czechs were to pay the price for the humiliating killing of Heydrich. The most brutal punishment was meted out to the village of Lidice, which was burnt to the ground with all adult male villagers being killed. Women were sent along with the children to concentration camps where they were gassed with a few 'Aryan' looking children put out for adoption by German couples. (*Author's Collection, Public Domain*)

Partisan activity in the Czech Protectorate of Bohemia and Moravia was difficult due to a lack of heavily forested areas and mountains where they could have established safe camps. This group of partisans are travelling over the border between the Czech Protectorate and Slovakia, where they hoped to find safer terrain in which to operate. They would now face the military forces of the pro-German Slovakian government led by Tiso, which saw the partisans as their bitter enemies. The ineffective Government Army of the Czech Protectorate, with only 7,000 men and limited to small arms only, had been given the role by the Germans of internal security. (*Author's Collection, Public Domain*)

The Honour Guard of the Government Army of the Protectorate of Bohemia and Moravia take the salute outside the HQ of the Emil Hacha regime in 1940. This puppet administration was allowed by the German occupiers to raise a very limited military force of less than 7,000 men in July 1939. Its personnel were issued only with Vz.24 rifles and their sole role was internal security within the protectorate. Some of its men were sent to Northern Italy to fight partisans in the spring of 1944 but were soon brought home. (*Author's Collection, Public Domain*)

(**Above**) This post-war mock-up shows three Czech partisans with a background of the mountains that they operated from during 1943–45. The earliest partisan activity involved small groups like this who had evaded arrest after Heydrich's assassination in May 1942 and took shelter in the Moravian Mountain range. In early 1942 the first documented partisan group was operating in the Hoytyn-Vsetin Mountains on the Czech-Slovak border. (*Author's Collection, Public Domain*)

(**Opposite, above**) This group of Jan Zizka partisans includes Dayan Bajanovic Murzin, the Chief of Staff of the Brigade, in the centre with hands on hip. These men belong to a unit of the brigade which tried to cross the Slovak-Moravian border on 22 September 1944. This attempt was unsuccessful and it was decided to send smaller groups into Moravia. The first group which managed to cross the border undetected to start a partisan campaign in Moravia was only sixty fighters strong. (*Author's Collection, Public Domain*)

(**Below**) Vilem Kantor and Karel Votalik of the 1st Jan Zizky Brigade are seen during training in the summer of 1944. The young age of these two fighters was not unusual among the partisans with one veteran recalling that he was 17 when he joined the brigade. His friends who fought beside him were two older boys of 18, and two 16 year olds who fought well. These young men didn't have the same responsibilities as older fighters and were said to have taken more risks than their comrades. (*Author's Collection. Public Domain*)

(**Above**) The command of the 1st Czechoslovak Jan Zizka Brigade show off their newly made banner to their fighters. It is adorned with the hammer and sickle symbol of the Soviet Union on one side, and on the other the white lion of Bohemia. In the centre of the flag is an image of the one-eyed Jan Zizka, a thirteenth- and fourteenth-century hero who was a follower of Jan Hus. Hus was the leader of the Hussites who fought against the Teutonic Order and the forces of the Holy Roman Empire in the early 1400s. (*Author's Collection, Public Domain*)

(**Left**) This is Hans Kocher, commander of the Jan Ziska Brigade known by the nickname Schupo, who had previously served as a driver for the Holesav Battalion. He shows his authority not by any rank insignia but by his clothing and the weaponry he carries. His leather jacket was favoured by irregular commanders throughout the twentieth century and his fur hat would be useful in the Czechoslovakian winter. Despite the shortage of arms in the Czech guerrilla forces he has a PPSH-41 submachine gun and a CZ 27 automatic pistol. (*Private Collection, Public Domain*)

Leaders of the Jan Zizka Brigade pose for the camera with Commander Dajan Bajanovic Murzin in the centre with leather hat. The brigade was the strongest partisan formation in the Czechoslovakian regions of Bohemia and Moravia during the Second World War. A lack of arms for the partisans was a major issue until the Soviet Red Army began supplying them with small arms in the last months of the war. Weapons like the German MP-40 were usually kept in the hands of the partisan leaders, while the rank and file had to share the ex-Czech rifles between them. (*Author's Collection, Public Domain*)

A column of the Jan Ziska Partisan Brigade partisans march through a town recently liberated from the German Army. The arms carried by the partisans include a Czech ZB-30 light machine and a Bren gun, the British modification of the ZB-30. Most of the column are armed with captured Mauser rifles or the Czech version of the rifle, the VZ-24. In August 1944 the brigade had been formed when a small group of Red Army trained Czech parachutists dropped into Moravia to form the core of the unit. (*Author's Collection, Public Domain*)

General Jan Golian (1906–1945) seen here in his Slovakian Army uniform was the first leader of the 1944 Slovak Uprising. He had been a Slovak Brigade Commander but decided to organise resistance to the German takeover of Slovakia in April 1944. Having taken command of the Slovakian resistance forces in Central Slovakia he established his HQ at the town of Banska Bystrica. Knowing that his limited forces could not hold out for more than fourteen days he decided to join up with other Slovak forces in the east of the country. When the uprising failed he and his replacement as Commander of Slovak forces, General Viest, were arrested by the German special forces and shot in Flossenbürg concentration camp in early 1945. (*Author's Collection, Public Domain*)

General Rudolf Viest (1890–1945) was the highest ranking Slovak in the pre-1938 Czechoslovak Republic's Army. Although he was a proud Slovak he was against the breakaway of Slovakia in March 1939. For a while he served as inspector-general of the Slovak Army, but eventually escaped to France in September 1939. When the Slovak Uprising began in April 1944 he left his position in the Czechoslovak government-in-exile. At the urgings of General Golian he returned to Slovakia on 7 October to take over command of the uprising. He and General Golian worked closely together but the uprising was failing and their joint last order on 27 October was for all Slovak troops to be come guerrillas. Viest was arrested along with General Golian, sharing his fate in Flossenburg camp sometime in early 1945. (*Author's Collection, Public Domain*)

Slovakian partisans along with some Slovakian troops march towards the front line of the uprising in the last days of August 1944. The estimates of the number of partisans who joined the uprising vary greatly with the highest saying that 27,400 fought. Many of these fighters were in fact from the Slovakian Army, with 18,000 soldiers estimated to have joined the rebellion. The largest partisan unit, led by Lieutenant-Colonel Sukajev, had 7,000 members, while the smallest, led by Captain de Laurienne, had only 180 fighters. (*Author's Collection, Public Domain*)

Monsignor Jozef Tiso (1887–1947) a Slovak Catholic priest was the head of the Slovak People's Party pre-1938. After the German takeover of Czechoslovakia in 1938 he became the self-proclaimed leader of an autonomous Slovak Sate, which in March 1939 became an independent state. As the leader of a 'client' state of Nazi Germany, Tiso cooperated fully with the deportation of the Jewish population to be exterminated. In the summer of 1944 he was rewarded for his loyalty to Hitler by getting German support to crush the uprising in Slovakia. At the end of the war he fled the country and was arrested in Germany by US troops then sent back to Slovakia, where he was hanged in 1947 for treason. (*Author's Collection, Public Domain*)

(**Above, left**) Hlinka Guardsmen undergo training in 1944 having been issued with full Czech uniforms from the Slovak military stores. The Hlinka Guard was formed in 1938 and served the Tiso regime until the bitter end and were involved in deporting Jews during the war. In 1941 some guardsmen received military training from the SS and many middle-class members decided to leave the organisation. From 1941 until 1945 the core of the Hlinka Guard were made up of lower-class Slovaks, most of whom still fully supported the Tiso regime. About 8,000 guardsmen took part in the crushing of the Slovak Uprising alongside German units. (*Author's Collection, Public Domain*)

(**Above right**) This Slovak Tiso government poster is publicising 14 March as the day of the Hlinka Guard. Slovakian society was deeply divided during the Second World War and there was substantial support for this Fascist organisation. Anyone tainted by association with the Tiso government had reason to continue to support him, knowing their fate if it was overthrown. The flag of the Hlinka Guard was blue with a white circle and a red double cross, the symbol of Slovakia. (*Author's Collection, Public Domain*)

(**Opposite, above**) These Slovak rebels taking part in the Slovak National Rising (SNP) are fighting against the invading German Army and the forces of the client state of Tiso. Under the name of the 1st Czechoslovak Army in Slovakia, the rebel forces were made up largely of sections of the Slovakian Army. Formed in early October 1944, the rebel army established its headquarters in the town of Banska Bystrica. A total of 60,000 former Slovak soldiers joined the rebels and were supported by up to 18,000 partisans. (*Author's Collection, Public Domain*)

(**Opposite, below**) Two Slovak Air Force officers are in command of a unit of the 1st Czechoslovak Army and still wear their old uniforms. The officers are Captain Daniel Kunic and Captain Mikulasom Sumichrastom, who have left their squadron to command an infantry unit. There was little time to organise the anti-German forces and the determination by the Germans to crush the uprising soon affected the fighting ability of the poorly supplied rebel forces. (*Author's Collection, Public Domain*)

This determined looking group of fighters of the 1st Czechoslovak Army in Slovakia pose before going into battle against the Hlinka Guard and their German allies. Support for the rebels came not only from the Slovak partisans but also from the Red Army, which did supply some weaponry. After two months of fighting the rebels effectively ended fighting on 28 October after being outgunned by the tough German formations. Former Slovak soldiers like these usually joined the growing partisan forces in Slovakia and continued fighting the regime and the Germans until April 1945, when the Red Army 'liberated' the country. (*Author's Collection, Public Domain*)

The young Wallachian partisan leader in 1944 on the left of the photograph is Jan Manak from the town of Huslenek in Wallachian Moravia. He has been supplied by the Red Army with his PPSH-41 submachine gun, while the man in the centre has a Romanian Orita submachine gun. The young fighter on the right is armed with the Czech VZ-24 short rifle showing the wide variety of sources of arms in the Czech and Slovak resistance. (*Author's Collection, Public Domain*)

A Czech partisan anti-tank crew have dug into a position in the Tatra Mountains on the border between Slovakia and Poland. They are armed with a Soviet PTRS-41 anti-tank rifle which was produced in its hundreds of thousands during the Second World War. It could fire effectively up to 800m with a maximum range of 1,500m, and could be used against other targets beside armoured vehicles. By the time this photograph was taken in early 1945, the Red Army was supplying substantial armaments to the left-wing partisan groups in Czechoslovakia. (*Author's Collection*)

This group of Wallachian partisans are well armed with captured MP-40 submachine guns and at least one Soviet PPSH-41 submachine gun. The youth of the fighters is evident, and there is a single female who appears not to have been trusted with a firearm. Even though most partisan units throughout Europe were left-wing, women and girls were still expected to fill the roles of medical and administration duties. (*Author's Collection, Public Domain*)

Lieutenant Jan Nalepka of the pro-German Slovakian Army was the leader of a group of Slovak partisans. He had formed an underground anti-Fascist cell in the Slovakian Army serving on the Russian Front. In mid-June 1943 Nalepka and some fellow officers defected from the Slovak Army and joined the local partisans. They led a detachment of partisans calling for other Slovak soldiers to join them, and operated for five months before taking part in an attack against the town of Ovruch. Nalepka and most of his fellow officers were killed during the attack on 16 November and were buried in a mass grave. He became a hero in post-war Czechoslovakia where his hometown Smizany has a street and a school named after him. (*Author's Collection, Public Domain*)

Heavily armed ROA motorcyclists have their first encounter with Czech insurgents in the centre of Prague on 6 May. Once the insurgent leaders had established the Russians' motives they welcomed their help and the heavy weaponry, including Hetzer tank destroyers, they had brought with them. The Russians fought hard during the uprising and stormed the German positions alongside the Czechs, losing 300 men in the fighting. (*Author's Collection, Public Domain*)

This ROA soldier is surrounded by welcoming Prague women and children after his arrival in the city centre. The mood had drastically changed by the 7th, when it became apparent that the Red Army would soon be arriving in Prague. Czech left-wing insurgents disowned the Russians, despite the fact that the ROA had saved them from defeat and told them they were no longer considered allies. Although some Russians tried to escape towards American lines most were handed over to the vengeful Red Army when they arrived. Other insurgents pleaded with the Red Army to spare General Bunyachenko and his men but many were shot or sent back to the Soviet Union where the officers were hanged. (*National Archives*)

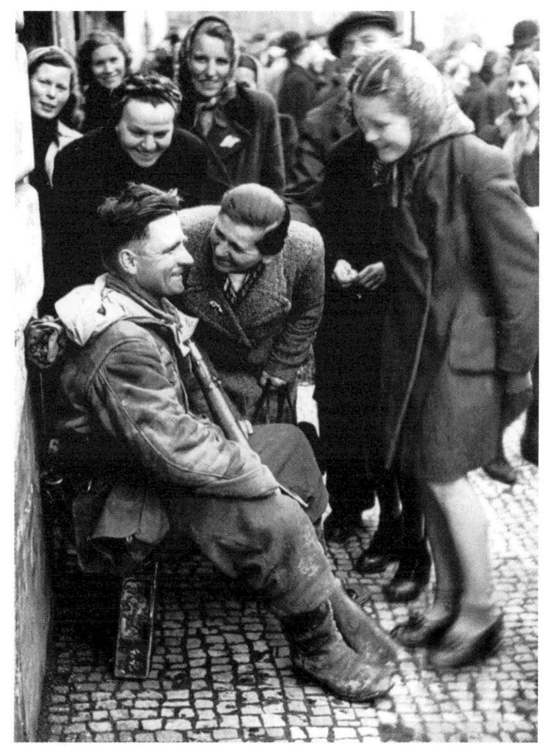

These men of the pro-German 'Russian Liberation Army' (ROA) pose with Prague citizens, who for a few days in early May 1945 regarded the Russians as liberators against the German Army. The commander of the ROA 1st Division, General Sergei Bunyachenko, had been ordered to take his men towards Prague to join up with German units, but he had other ideas. Although he did take the 1st Division to Prague he set his HQ in the city's suburbs and then marched his men into the centre to try to join the Czech insurgents. (*National Archives*)

Czech fighters man a barricade during the Prague Uprising; with few rifles and no heavy weaponry they were fighting a courageous but losing battle. The 30,000 Czech insurgents were not supported by the Red Army during the four day uprising and any weapons they had were taken from the enemy. These fighters are armed with rifles either German Mausers or Czech VZ-24s and a ZB-30 light machine gun. (*Author's Collection, Public Domain*)

A civilian fighter has managed to acquire a Mauser rifle and a single German type stick grenade with which to defend his barricade. He has also found a Czech M29 steel helmet with a metal comb on top and has decorated the front with a paper Czech flag. Rebels like this man could expect no mercy from the German governor of the Czech lands, Hans Frank, who said that the uprising would be met with a 'sea of blood'. (*Author's Collection, Public Domain*)

This photograph was taken in the course of the Prague Uprising and shows three insurgents manning a barricade. The man in the centre of the group is wearing an M16 steel helmet from the First World War which was used post-1918 by the Czech Army. He mans a captured MG-34 machine gun while his comrade in the foreground feeds strips of ammunition into it. Their comrade in the background is armed with a VZ-24 rifle as used by the Czechs up to 1938 and the Slovaks from 1939–44. (*Author's Collection, Public Domain*)

On 6 May, this pair of former French AMR 35 light tanks which were utilised by the German Army fell into the hands of insurgents. Twelve of these tanks had been used by the Germans in Panzerkampfwagen-Kompanie 539 for occupation duties in Prague. They have been positioned on Bartolomesjka Street in the centre of Prague and decorated with white paint for the CSR – Czech Socialist Republic. Whether the three captured tanks had much ammunition is doubtful, but their presence is intended to give the insurgents some hope in the uneven battle for the city. (*Author's Collection, Public Domain*)

This poor quality image from 1945 shows an unnamed female Czech partisan who is fighting in support of the Soviet Red Army in the last weeks of the war. She has been given a PPSH-41 submachine gun with the minimum of equipment and does not appear to have spare magazines. (*Author's Collection, Public Domain*)

Chapter Eight

Italian Partisans

Led by Benito Mussolini, Italy had been under Fascist rule since 1922 and all opposition had been ruthlessly crushed by the regime's secret police, the OVRA. Up to 50,000 OVRA operatives kept the population in line, although many Italians enthusiastically supported the government. During the mid- to late 1930s Mussolini increasingly found himself outshone on the world stage by his fellow Fascist leader in Germany, Adolf Hitler. Hitler had been an admirer of Mussolini during his early political career but by the late 1930s the Italian dictator was in the shadow of the more ruthless and astute German leader. With a struggling economy and the beginnings of waning support, Mussolini decided on an aggressive foreign policy. In 1935 he launched an invasion of Abyssinia, which ended in 1936 with the independent country becoming part of the Italian Empire. His support of the right-wing rebellion in Spain from 1936 to 1939 drained the Italian economy and expended much of Italy's military resources. The decade ended with the Italian takeover of the impoverished client state of Albania, which again was added to the Italian Empire in April 1939. Pragmatically, Mussolini did not rush to join Germany in its war with the British and France after their invasion of Poland in September 1939. After Germany's startling victories in Scandinavia and then the Low Countries and France, he decided to jump before Hitler had taken all the spoils. Mussolini's ill fated declaration of war against the Allies led to a series of disastrous military campaigns between June 1940 and July 1943. The end of the North African Campaign was followed by the invasion of the Italian island of Sicily. When Sicily fell it was only a matter of time before the Allies invaded Italy and the Italian dictator's demise was certain to follow. Opposition in Italy to Mussolini had been growing since 1940, with Communist cells existing in many factories. Some left-wing workers began to gather arms and carried out raids on Fascist targets at night and at the weekend. The overthrow of Mussolini was swiftly followed by the German takeover of Italy and the disarming of Italian troops during September 1943. Codenamed 'Operation Achse', the brutal methods used by the Germans in subduing any opposition to their takeover turned some previously pro-Axis people into the opposition ranks.

Underground anti-Fascist forces came into the open after 8 September 1943, although there had previously been a low level of sabotage and other activities by Communists and Socialists. Some had fought on the Republican side during the Spanish Civil War 1936–39 and these brought their experience into the emerging partisan movement. During 'Operation Achse' a number of Italian troops resisted the enemy both in Italy and in the Balkans but were overwhelmed by the superior weaponry of the Germans. Up to 45,000 Italian personnel were killed in resisting the Germans and 700,000 troops were interned, with up to 50,000 dying during their captivity. Another source of opposition to the German occupation was the young men who were now being pressed into working for the Germans in their industry. Many of these youths and men now 'took to the hills' and joined the early partisan groups who took shelter in the forests and mountains of Italy.

After the Allied invasion of Italy the Communist leadership agreed to cooperate with the new pro-Allied Badoglio government in the south, and support the country's monarchy. Also in support of the Allies were other political factions such as the 'Action Party' and the Socialists. Armed groups emerged but were at first stifled by the German occupation of the majority of Italy. Between September and October 1943 it was estimated that there were 1,500 partisans in Italy, with two thirds of them in the north. By December 1943 the number of partisans had grown to about 10,000 fighters as they were joined by a large number of youths who were trying to avoid conscription by the Fascists into the various militias and paramilitaries. By April 1944 there were 13,500 partisans, of which 48 per cent were Communists. These partisans were distributed through Central and Northern Italy with 3,500 in the North-Western Alps. There were about 1,500 men in the vicinity of both Milan and Genoa, and another 2,000 were in the north-east.

Most partisans fought from 1943 to 1945 under the umbrella anti-Fascist organisation, the 'National Liberation Committee'. The most dominant partisan forces belonged to the Communist Brigate Garibaldi, or Garibaldi Brigades. Other large partisan groups included the 'Justice & Freedom Brigades', whose fighters were affiliated to the Partito d'Azione or Action Party, and the 'Matteotti Brigades' whose fighters were followers of the Socialist Party. One smaller partisan organisation which came under CLN control was affiliated to the Christian Democrat Party. The Garibaldi Brigades made up 41 per cent of the 80,000 active partisans while the Justice & Freedom Brigades made up 29 per cent.

Operating outside the control of the 'National Liberation Committee' were a host of smaller partisan groups like the Monarchist 'Green Flame Brigades' and the 'Clandestine Military Front', which was commanded by Colonel Montezemolo. Competition from the Left Wing to the Communist Garibaldi Brigades came from Anarchist partisans and dissident Communists who belonged the large armed group the 'Movimento Comunista d'Italia'. Other groups included the 'Fronte Militare Clandestino', which was headed by Colonel Motezemolo and the 'Autonomous Partisans' (Autonomi), which were made up of former Italian Army soldiers. The Autonomi group had no political alignment, with its fighters united only by their hatred of the Germans. These fighters were particularly bitter about the German 'Operation Achse' in September 1943, which saw the Italian Army swiftly disbanded, often brutally, by the German forces in Italy.

The first success of partisan forces took place at the end of September 1943 when, during the 'Four Days of Naples', they liberated the Southern city. Although the Naples resistance had taken the important city in this spontaneous uprising, elsewhere in Central and Northern Italy the partisans were struggling to survive during the winter of 1943–44. The various independent and isolated partisan groups in late 1943 and early 1944 were suffering from a chronic shortage of central control. In an effort to rectify this lack of control, Italian Army General Raffaele Cadorna[*] was parachuted into Northern Italy to take command. Arriving with him were his two chiefs of staff, a Communist named Longo and Ferrucio Parri, a member of the liberal Action Party. By June 1944 some larger groups were able to support the Allied offensive towards Rome, which fell that month. By late 1944 the various partisan groups had reached a strength of 85,000 men, and with arms dropped by Allied planes they were able to take on German and Fascist Italian forces. The Germans were pleased when the Italian partisans came out into the open to fight in the summer of 1944, it gave the occupiers a target that they could attack.

---

* The son of First World War Italian marshal, Luigi Cadorna.

(**Above**) A section of partisans of the 36th Garibaldi Brigade are on patrol in the Tosco-Ramognolo mountains, part of the Apennines range. Although partisans organised all over occupied Italy in the summer of 1943, many were ex-Soldiers of the Italian 4th Army. These men had been withdrawing from Southern France into Piedmont province when many decided to join the resistance or form their own partisan units. The number of partisans on the strength of each partisan unit fluctuated from one month to another. For instance, one Garibaldi Brigade had only thirty men in January 1944, but by February there were 3,000 in its ranks. A month later this brigade had been reduced again, but this time only down to 600 men. (*Author's Collection, Public Domain*)

(**Opposite, above**) Two Italian civilians begin resistance to the German occupation of Italy by preparing explosives to use against units moving through Northern Italy. These early partisans were joined by Italian soldiers who were avoiding being conscripted by the Germans. At the same time, the left-wingers who had long opposed Mussolini now came out into the open to resist the Germans and the 'puppet' Salo Republic. (*Author's Collection, Public Domain*)

(**Opposite, below**) This small group of partisans are typical of the first armed forces that identified themselves as anti-Fascist fighters in the summer of 1943. Organised in the days and weeks after the German occupation of Italy, these men are in their own clothes which would soon wear out. They have, however, been supplied with a US Thompson submachine gun, a British Lee Enfield .303 rifle and a Bren gun. (*Author's Collection, Public Domain*)

In the very early days of resistance to the German occupation of their country, small groups of mostly young men headed into the hills of mountains of Italy. Many were trying to avoid being coerced into volunteering as workers to go to Germany to help the war industry. These young men including one wearing the hat of an Alpini mountain soldier have a couple of Mannlicher Carcano M1891 rifles between them. They are camping in the hills above their town and will probably join an organised partisan group in due course. (*Author's Collection*, *Public Domain*)

In the early days of the German occupation of Italy in September 1943, a unit of paratroopers have organised a couple of Italian crewed L3/35 tankettes to help them deal with anti-German elements. Over the next almost two years Italy was deeply divided between the pro- and anti-Fascists, with some Italians staying loyal to Mussolini. Others chose a different path and actively resisted the Fascist Republic at Salo and the German occupiers. (*Author's Collection*, *Public Domain*)

This Italian partisan has been captured in an ambush by German troops near Abruzzi and is to be given the expected swift justice. The original caption says that the brave man watches serenely as the German troops tie him to a tree in preparation for his death by firing squad. (*Author's Collection, Public Domain*)

(**Above**) Some of these left-wing partisans are making their political affiliation clear by pinning red stars to the front of their hats or on their shirts or tunics. Although the political rivalry between the various partisan groups in Italy was not as vicious as in some occupied country's there was little love lost between them. This group are operating in the Romagna region and have received a number of British Sten submachine guns to go with their captured Italian weapons. (*Author's Collection, Public Domain*)

(**Opposite, above**) Three partisans of a Garibaldi Brigade pose for the camera in the town of Urbino on 9 September 1944. The town had been liberated on 28 August by a combination of Polish troops of the British 'V' Corps and Italian partisan forces. During the battle for Urbino the Germans captured a number of partisans who were executed on the Punto Panoramica bridge. (*Author's Collection*)

(**Opposite, below**) This unit of the 36th Garibaldi Brigade poses for a typical group photograph showing the clothing and weaponry of the Italian partisans. Unfortunately for the partisans, the winter of 1944–45 was a harsh one and light clothing like this would have to be substituted by greatcoats and any other suitable winter wear. (*Author's Collection*)

(**Above**) These men belong to the 36th Brigade of the Garibaldini in 1944 and this unit had received arms from OSS, which had been air dropped to them from Allied transports. The 36th was reported to be a disciplined 1,200 strong unit and it was commanded by an ex-Italian Army artillery lieutenant who had the nom-de-guerre 'Bob'. (*Author's Collection, Public Domain*)

(**Opposite, above**) Jewish partisans pose in the Italian mountains while fighting alongside their Christian comrades in 1944. Some were escaping from the attentions of the Germans and had nothing to lose by fighting with the partisans. Many had come to Italy having fled Nazi-occupied Europe and, before 1943, had found that most Italians were not inherently antisemitic. Other Jews who fought with partisans in Russia and Poland still found the deep-seated dislike of the Jewish faith among the population and in their units. (*Author's Collection, Public Domain*)

(**Opposite, below**) Maggiorino Marcellin (Blute-Butler) the commander of partisan formations in the Chisone Valley near Turin poses with his arm around a younger fighter. He came from a very poor background and his father had to emigrate to France because of his opposition to Mussolini. Maggiorino became a ski instructor while travelling to and from France establishing contacts with the anti-fascist opposition. As with many partisans he served during the Second World War, in his case during the 1940–41 Greek Campaign. From 1943 he established partisans forces forming the 1st Autonomous Alpine Division. During fighting against Fascist forces he was wounded twice and was decorated with the Partisan Silver Medal. (*Author's Collection, Public Domain*)

Lieutenant Aldo Gastaldi 'Bisagno' seen in reflective mood was the commander of Garibaldi units in Liguria. As with most partisans who lived in Italy in 1940 he was called up to the army and served in the Engineers. In 1943 he was contacted by members of the Communist Party who knew his political sympathies. They proposed he set up a partisan group which soon became the 'Chichero' Partisan Division which operated in the mountains around the city of Genoa. He was known as one of the best, most feared and most refuted partisan leaders, but died in May 1945 in a motor accident, after falling from the roof of a truck cab. (*Author's Collection, Public Domain*)

(**Opposite, above**) Four members of the command staff of a large partisan unit pose in the centre of Florence on 4 August 1944. The partisans around the city belonged largely to the Tuscan Committee of National Liberation (CTNL), which had been founded in October 1943. As the Allied armies began to converge on Florence the CTNL began a series of actions against the German garrison holding the city. They were in the city when the 6th South African Division broke through the last defences, while the partisans were in the process of destroying the remaining pockets of resistance. (*Author's Collection, Public Domain*)

(**Opposite, below**) Bogliolo, holding the battered motorcycle, was one of the most active and authoritarian leaders of the partisans in the Langhe Region. The partisans set up a number of free republics, including the Republic of Langhe, which survived from September to November 1944. These republics were often just a group of villages or towns, and when attacked by German and Fascist artillery and armour, their defenders usually withdrew into the hills and mountains. (*Author's Collection, Public Domain*)

Partisans of one of the better dressed and equipped groups pose in a studio for a group photograph. Some of the older partisans had been members of left-wing parties before the rise of Mussolini in 1921. Most, however, had grown up under the Fascist regime and although indoctrinated by its propaganda machine had rejected its policies and had waited for the day when they could fight against it. (*Author's Collection*)

This unit of partisans is operating between the towns Sestri Levante in the Western Alps, and Chiavari in Liguria province in north-west Italy. Second from right in this group is the local partisan leader Paolo Castagnino, known as 'Saetta' or 'Lightning', who was also a well known folk singer. The partisan movement was full of liberal-minded people like Castagnino who had been stifled by the twenty or more years of Fascist rule. Clothing worn by this group of fighters is quite eclectic with one wearing a straw boater and another what appears to be a cowboy hat. (*Author's Collection*)

A partisan officer belonging to the Garibaldi Brigades and has the rank of a detachment commander on the left chest of his pullover smock. The smock probably belonged to one of the elite formations of the pre-1943 army and it was popular with partisans when they could acquire one. (*Author's Collection*)

A group of Garibaldini partisans are photographed in the Val d'Ossola where a number of their units operated. The valley and seven valleys that ran off it was in the province of Verbano-Cusio-Ossola in the Piedmont region. For a short period from 8 September to 23 October 1944 the valley was the centre of the Free Republic of Ossola. Switzerland gave this short lived republic official recognition before it was attacked by gathering enemy forces. It was one of the partisan republics which was formed during the summer and autumn of 1944 but all had been destroyed by the Germans and Italian Fascists within a few months. (*Author's Collection*)

(**Above**) These men belong to one of the 'Justice & Liberty' partisan groups, raised mainly from members of the Action Party. The 'Justice & Liberty' Liberal-Socialist movement had been one of the most active anti-Fascist organisations during the late 1920s onwards. In 1942 the Action Party was formed and its armed wing was in a loose alliance with the stronger Garibaldini partisan groups. In reality the only thing the two groups had in common was their opposition to Mussolini and the Salo Republic from 1943. (*Author's Collection, Public Domain*)

(**Opposite, above**) Happy Italian partisans of an unknown group pose with their recently acquired Sten MkII submachine guns. From 1943 until the end of the war in Italy in May 1945 there was no shortage of willing volunteers to fight the German occupation. When arms air drops began, partisan groups sprang up all over Central and Northern Italy to fight the German occupiers and the forces of the Salo Republic. (*Author's Collection, Public Domain*)

(**Opposite, below**) A unit of partisans take part in a parade after liberating a village in the Apennines. The variety of weaponry on display shows that the Italian partisans had to arm themselves with a mixture of captured German-Italian guns and weapons given to them by the Allies. In the front row two machine gunners are armed with a British Bren gun and a German MG-34 light machine gun. (*Author's Collection, Public Domain*)

Three partisans of the 12th Garibaldi Brigade 'Copelli' Detachment pose with their two Carcano carbines and a Sten MKII submachine gun. The men are from left to right; Manfredo Lezzi (who died on 10 July 1944) Francisco Panini 'Cecco', and Celso Lugli 'Sergeant'. (*Author's Collection, Public Domain*)

An Italian partisan who is attached to the Co-Belligerent 'Cremona' Battle Group is armed with a captured MP40 Maschinenpistole 40 submachine gun. The pro-Allied 'Cremona' had a strength of 9,000 men and local partisans like this man would volunteer to perform roles for them. He has been issued with British battledress and a beret with a tricolour ribbon attached and has the shoulder title 'partisan' and '8a', presumably for 8th Army, sewn on the tunic. (*Author's Collection, Public Domain*)

Partisans rest between operations and familiarise themselves with a British supplied 3in mortar. Heavy weaponry was in short supply with the partisans, even though many ex-Italian arms were available in 1943. Anti-tank weapons must have included PIAT anti-tank launchers but there are few if any images of these in use with the Italian partisans. Most enemy armoured vehicles, according to reports, were destroyed by anti-tank grenades rather than by bazookas or PIATs. (*Author's Collection, Public Domain*)

Partisans of the Garibaldini pose confidently and show off their weaponry to the international press. The average age of an Italian partisan fighter was between 19 and 24, with many being 17 or even younger. Younger partisans like these lacked any real practical military training and relied on their more experienced comrades to teach them. It was difficult to command young fighters like these who were in a rebellious mood after growing up in the restrictive society of Fascist Italy. Headgear worn by this group include a British beret, an army peaked cap and even helmet liners all adorned by the standard red star. (*Author's Collection, Public Domain*)

(**Above**) These partisans look like bandits from the Renaissance period of history, apart from the modern weapons slung over their shoulders. They are operating in support of the Allies around Cisterna in Cassino Province during the summer of 1944. The long haired partisan is armed with a German Macshinenkarabiner 42H, while the man in the centre has a Sten MkII, and on the right the partisan is armed with a German MP-40. (*Author's Collection, Public Domain*)

(**Opposite, above**) This group of unknown partisans are typical of the demographic make-up of the anti-Fascist fighters. Many had been too young to fight when war broke out in 1940, and as the war went badly for Italy few wanted to join up. To avoid conscription thousands 'took to the hills' and found shelter with armed groups already forming in the mountains. Of course they were expected to fight for their hosts and many willingly fought against the German Occupiers and Italian Fascists. (*Author's Collection, Public Domain*)

(**Opposite, below**) A young woman partisan who had been a schoolteacher moves through deep snow in the mountains around Aosta in the winter of 1944–45. She carries what appears to be a 9mm Suomi M31 submachine gun which was designed and produced in Finland in the 1930s. This gun was also produced under licence in Switzerland and it must have been from this source that the partisans bought this weapon. Women were vital to the partisan struggle, with one unit having eighty females in its 200 strong unit. As one woman fighter said: 'It seemed absurd and impossible to stay bent over a table ten hours a day, to gossip with friends, while the Germans walked the streets, while the Fascists arrested young men.' (*Author's Collection*)

(**Above**) A group of partisans operating in the Val d'Aosta region during the winter of 1944–45 have found a comrade lost in a snow storm. The rugged terrain and harsh weather conditions were difficult for the partisans to operate in, but at least it gave them relief from the pressure of fighting German and Italian forces. (*Author's Collection, Public Domain*)

(**Left**) This group of fifteen partisans under the command of Scevola Franiosi move through the streets of Cesena in the Emilia Romagna region in Northern Italy on 20 October 1944. The town was situated close to the German 'Gothic Line' defensive lines and was heavily bombed during the war. These men are looking for signs of the Germans who still had some tanks in the town when the Canadians moved into the town to liberate it the same day. (*Author's Collection, Public Domain*)

This typical Italian partisan from an unknown group is wearing a mix of civilian and military clothing, including a scarf for the winter conditions. Although the partisans relied on captured uniforms or clothing handed over by sympathetic Italian troops, they soon added their own insignia. He is armed with a Carcano carbine with something carved into its stock, and he has a bandolier of spare six-bullet clips attached to his 'Mexican' style bandolier. (*Author's Collection, Public Domain*)

A young partisan from the Modena Apennines is pictured with his newly acquired US Thompson submachine gun manufactured in England. The average age of a partisan was between 19 and 24, although the general age group of volunteers was 17 to 35. Many were described as 'unruly' and unwilling to take orders from their older and senior comrades. (*Author's Collection, Public Domain*)

Chapter Nine

Italian Partisans & Fascists

After being overthrown by his own political allies on 25 July 1943, the Italian leader Benito Mussolini was taken 'for his own' safety to the island of Ponza. He was later transferred to a remote ski hotel at Grand Sasso from where he was rescued by commandos on 12 September on the orders of Hitler. Following an emotional meeting in Germany on the 15th, plans were put in place to restore Mussolini to power. The Italian dictator was duly installed as 'puppet' leader of the newly established 'Italian Social Republic' (RSI) in North-Eastern Italy on the 23rd. Armed forces quickly raised from among 'loyal' Italians to support the RSI were certainly impressive on paper. Four Divisions of the 'National Republican Army' (ENR) were raised from among the hundreds of thousands of Italian troops held in camps by the Germans after September 1943.

Although only one in ten of these troops volunteered to fight for Mussolini there were enough men to form four divisions in October 1943. These were the 1st 'Bersaglieri' Division, the 2nd 'Grenadier' Division, the 3rd Marine 'San Marco' Division and the 4th Alpini 'Monterosa' Division. These divisions, plus a number of attached autonomous units, totalled an impressive 300,000 men. In addition to the ENR there was the 'National Republican Guard' (GNR), which replaced the Carabinieri, Gendarmerie, and other police forces, with a strength of 140,000 men. In late June 1944, the still loyal Fascists who had served in the militia (MVSN) were formed into the 'Corpo Ausiliario delle Squadre d'Azione di Camicie Nere'. The units of the new militia were called Brigate Nere (Black Brigades), and totalled 110,000 men, women and youths. These brigades were often made up of older veterans of the Fascist Party and younger enthusiastic Fascists who were still loyal to Mussolini. All of the forty Brigate Nere and nine Mobile Brigades were named after Fascist heroes from the 1922–44 period.

In addition to the ENR, GNR and Brigate Nere, there were a number of independent formations including the elite 'X'' MAS'. This was a successor to the Naval Unit, which performed commando-type operations before the Armistice using midget submarines and fast attack boats. In RSI service the 'X" MAS', with a strength of 18,000 under the command of Junio Valerio Borghese, performed mainly anti-partisan operations with some success. On paper these forces raised by the RSI and the Socialist Republic were impressive, but they were not to prove as useful to the Germans as they had hoped. The early RSI forces proved to be ineffective in many cases and did not mount any major operations against their partisan enemies. Their main operations were limited to company-strong attacks with a total of 178 anti-partisan attacks taking place between December 1943 and February 1944. These resulted in the elimination of 254 partisans and the capture of another 200, whose fate is not known. ENR units were not trusted by their German allies and although trained to fight, other regular forces were often sent against partisans instead.

The RSI regular forces did fight against the US Army in the winter of 1944, when a regimental sized force defeated the Americans. They also fought against the growing Yugoslav partisan forces on the border of Yugoslavia and North-Eastern Italy in early 1945. Attempts were made to improve the performance of all the RSI regular and irregular forces with Cacciatori degli Appennini (Apennine Hunters) raising 10,000 men. Four regiments of the 'Apennine Hunters', 1st, 2nd, 3rd and 4th, were trained from early 1944 and sent against the partisans while still undergoing training. Despite losing some elements to the ENR during 1944 these units gained a good reputation and continued to fight until May 1945. Other 'elite' units included men who had fought on the Eastern Front as part of the Armata Italiana in Russia (ARMIR) between 1941 and April 1943. Having left 114,520 dead comrades in Russia, some of these men returned to Italy as tough and experienced veterans.

Behind German and Fascist Italian lines in Northern Italy during the civil war which existed from late 1943 until May 1945, a number of 'independent' short-lived republics were established by the partisans. These republics usually set up their own administration with free elections and taxation and price controls enforced by the partisans. The first republic was the Republic of Corniolo, formed in February 1944 and lasting a month before being overrun by German troops. In north-western Italy there was the Ossola Republic, which existed from 10 September until 23 October. It was defended by several partisan formations including three divisions and three Garibaldi Brigades, a Matteotti Brigade and the Beltrami Brigade. The Republic of Alto Monterrato was defended by two partisan Divisions: the VIII and the IX, and the II and V Garibaldi Brigades. In total there were twenty of these republics established with some controlling a few villages while others contained several large towns. Throughout the summer, autumn and early winter these republics were organised and then usually defeated by strong Italian Fascist and German forces. Although the Germans could have left these liberated zones to their own devices they decided to crush them, and were usually successful. When the well-armed German units withdrawn from the front line attacked the republics there was little that the partisans could do. Although the republics failed in some aspects, they did tie down German and Fascist forces with heavy weaponry – troops that could have been facing the Allied advance. Any partisan forces that were pushed out of these republics usually returned to their mountain bases where they continued their struggle into 1945.

In May 1945 the partisans again came back into play, aiding the Allies in taking charge of the 40,000 German and Italian Fascist prisoners. They also managed to stop the Germans from destroying many bridges and other infrastructure, including telegraph and telephone poles. Partisan groups took control of over a hundred urban centres, having liberated them before the Allied Army arrived. They also took control of much of the captured military equipment – which they didn't get to use as their forces were disbanded soon after the German surrender. The fate of the Italian Fascist prisoners left in partisan hands was usually severe with officers and political leaders, and even famous pro-Fascist film stars, swiftly executed. Besides a number of Mussolini's henchmen the most prized victim for the partisans was the Italian leader himself. He was captured by partisans, kept in custody overnight and then taken out and shot by the shore of Lake Como, along with his latest mistress Claretta Petacci. The Italian partisans were without doubt a great help to the Allied armies advancing through Italy from 1943 until 1945. Their presence certainly aided the British 8th and US 5th Army and speeded up their advance from central into Northern Italy.

(**Opposite, above**) Men of the X MAS Marine Division of the Italian Army of the Salo Republic parade through an Italian town to show the population that Mussolini is still in charge. They carry the flag of the Army of the Salo Republic and have the distinctive insignia of the X MAS on their uniforms. In reality, Mussolini was kept in power in Northern Italy mainly by the forces of his fellow Fascist dictator Adolf Hitler. (*Author's Collection, Public Domain*)

(**Opposite, below**) There were a number of uniformed formations raised in the support of the RSI from 1943, with the Salo Republic also having a female organisation. These young women belong to the Ausiliare, which was intended to support the fighting men of the regular army, GNR and Black Brigades. Although these women are armed they were not intended to fight while their fellow females in the Brigate Nere did take part in fighting against the partisans until the end of the war. (*Author's Collection, Public Domain*)

(**Above**) Men of the Brigate Nere set up an anti-aircraft machine gun on the wagon of a train which will be moving through countryside where partisans operate. The Brigate Nere were set up in August 1944 and its personnel were a mix of older MVSN Fascists and younger 'patriotic' volunteers. Each brigade adopted their own insignia and arm shields, and units varied greatly in size but were usually led by a former MVSN leader. (*Author's Collection, Public Domain*)

(**Opposite, above**) This group of Brigate Nere volunteers have been given the task of patrolling the banks of a northern Italian river. The officer appears to belong to the GNR and is wearing the black shirt of the pre-1943 MVSN. All the other men have only black shirts which they are wearing with military khaki trousers, and three of the men are wearing Greek steel helmets. These were captured by the Italians and Germans during their 1940–41 campaigns against the Greek Army. (*Author's Collection, Public Domain*)

(**Opposite, below**) Crews of the Leonessa armoured unit give the Fascist salute with their MVSN daggers in front of their L3/35 tankettes in July 1944. These small tanks were obsolete in 1940 when they faced the British Army in Libya and should have been taken out of service. Those that were taken out of Italian service were seen during the rest of the Second World War in service with various client states like Croatia. In an anti-partisan role they were just about viable, but only to give covering fire with their twin fiat machine guns during an operation. (*Author's Collection, Public Domain*)

(**Above**) Marines of the RSI San Marco Infantry Division bring in two partisans captured during a sweep of the mountains in early 1944. The San Marco Division had been raised in late 1943 from sailors in the Italian Navy in the Aegean Sea with the addition of 400 Black Shirts. Only 1,800 of the men in the division had belonged to the pre-1943 formation of the Italian Royal Navy. By November 1943 the San Marco had 14,000 men, most of whom were ardent supporters of Mussolini and the Fascist government. Having undergone training in Germany the unit became one of the most capable anti-partisan formations in the RSI's Armed Forces. (*Author's Collection, Public Domain*)

(**Opposite, above**) These men belong to the Autonomous Police Mobile Legion 'Ettori Muti', named after Mussolini's bodyguard and intrepid pilot of Fascist propaganda fame. It was raised in September 1943 as a squad, but by July 1944 it was given the title of legion, with 1,500 officers and men. The Ettore Muti was a heavily armed police force which acted on the orders of the internal security forces of the Salo Republic. (*Author's Collection, Public Domain*)

(**Below**) Paratroopers of the 1st Battalion of the Folgore Regiment prepare to go out on anti-partisan operation in Piedmont in December 1944. The Folgore had been an Italian air force until pre-1943 and fought alongside the Germans from 1944. It fought mainly in the anti-partisan role and was made up of hardcore Fascists and young recruits loyal to Mussolini. (*Author's Collection, Public Domain*)

(**Above**) Fascist Militiamen of the Ettore Muti Autonomous Legion march through the streets of Milan in the summer of 1944. These young men would have served in the various youth groups of the Mussolini regime in the 1930s and early 1940s. Italy was deeply divided in 1943 when the dictator was overthrown and many Italians celebrated his downfall. Other Italians, especially in Northern Italy were still fanatically loyal to Mussolini and joined anti-Communist units like the Ettore Muti. (*Author's Collection, Public Domain*)

(**Opposite, above**) A German soldier and a Fascist Brigate Nere volunteer chat in a town in the Friuli Venezia-Guilia region of North Eastern Italy. The Brigate Nere were the post-1943 successors to the MVSN Black Shirts and its volunteers were still fanatically loyal to Benito Mussolini. Italy was divided into two bitterly opposite armed camps with no quarter given on either side during the last year of the Second World War. (*Author's Collection, Public Domain*)

(**Below**) Volunteers of one of the Brigate Nere formed to support the Mussolini-led government at Salo pose for a photograph. The official name for the Fascist militia was, 'Il Corpo Ausiliaro delle Squadre d'Azione de Camicie Nere', or 'Auxiliary Corps of the Black Shirts Action Squads'. These brigades were raised locally, often under the same leaders who had commanded the original pre-1943 Black Shirts. This unit has been formed in Pavia to the south of Milan to fight against any local partisan groups of whatever political allegiance. (*Author's Collection*)

(**Opposite, above**) A mortar team of the Guardia Nazionale Repubblicana (GNR) fires from a farmhouse towards partisan positions during the 1943–45 civil war in Italy. The GNR was intended to replace most of the pre-1943 security forces which had included the Carabinieri and Frontier Guards. With a strength of 140,000 men the GNR was at the forefront of the anti-partisan campaign until the end of the war in May 1945. (*Author's Collection, Public Domain*)

(**Opposite, below left**) The Under Secretary of the Salo Republic Navy, Admiral Guiseppe Graziani, inspects a unit of the Decima Flottiglia X MAS. Until 1943 this marine commando unit had specialised in underwater and surface attacks on Allied shipping. In September 1943 some of the men in the unit formed a pro-Mussolini force at the Naval base at La Spezia to fight partisans. It reached a strength of 18,000 men and was one of the foremost anti-partisan forces, fighting alongside German forces under the command of SS-General Karl Wolff. The admiral is talking to a young mascot of the unit who is fully armed and as equipped as his adult comrades. (*Author's Collection, Public Domain*)

(**Opposite, below right**) Two militiamen of an Italian Battaglioni M are seen before going into action in their field grey-green uniforms, with camouflage covering on their M35 helmets. Every M Battalion was made up of three companies of assault troops and a scout platoon. They had some heavy weaponry, including 81mm mortars and 47mm anti-tank guns which could be used as infantry support guns. These men formed a large part of the anti-partisan forces available to the Salo Republic from 1943 until the end of the war in May 1945. (*Author's Collection, Public Domain*)

In the centre of this group is an officer of the Italian Decima Flottiglia X MAS anti-partisan unit who is consulting with his allies from the German Army in Northern Italy. German officers respected many of the men of the Salo Republic's Army, especially those in elite units like the 'Decima Mas'. The Italian unit was commanded by Captain Junio Valerio Borghese, known as the 'Black Prince', a longstanding and loyal Fascist who offered his services to Germany in September 1943. The unit was active from October 1943 and was allowed a great deal of independence by the Germans due to their recognition of its performance and loyalty to Mussolini. (*Author's Collection, Public Domain*)

(**Above, left**) A German soldier shouts to his comrades during a search for partisan hideouts in Northern Italy in the summer of 1944. By this stage in the Italian campaign the Germans and their Fascist allies were concentrating on keeping control of urban areas. They largely left the control of the countryside to the partisans, who were faced with attacks from Italian Fascist para-militaries and militia. (*Author's Collection, Public Domain*)

(**Above, right**) This stylishly posed photograph, taken by a propaganda photographer who was touring Northern Italy, shows a trio of German anti-partisan troops. The vast majority of fighting against the partisans was done by the various Italian Fascists groups. German troops were, however, withdrawn from the front line at times to deal with major threats against their defence of Italy in 1944 and early 1945. (*Author's Collection, Public Domain*)

(**Opposite**) German bicycle troops set off on an anti-partisan operation in the summer of 1944 and are being towed behind a staff car to take them up the mountainside. During the Italian Campaign of 1943–45 the German Army had to deal with the threat from large numbers of Italian partisans. At times German soldiers would be withdrawn from the front line and sent to aid the Italian Fascist forces of the Salo Republic in hunting down the partisans. (*NAC*)

(**Above**) A unit of Guardia Nazionale Repubblicana (GNR) which was a gendarmerie force of the Italian Social Republic created on 8 December 1943. It was raised to replace the pre-1943 Carabinieri and also acted as a Gendarmerie force while performing anti-partisan duties. The GNR had specialised units to deal with various roles including Railway, Harbour, Mountain & Forests, Frontier and Highway GNR, and had a total strength of 140,000 men. These men, however, are receiving instructions before going on an anti-partisan operation and some have camouflaged their helmets with foliage. (*Author's Collection, Public Domain*)

(**Opposite, above**) A patrol of the Cacciatori Degli Appennini – 'Hunters of the Appenines', are seen at rest during an anti-partisan operation. This 10,000 strong RSI formation was the only one recruited specifically to fight Italian partisans with three regiments raised on 1 April 1944. Two months later the Cacciatori lost 4,220 of their men who were forced to transfer to the RSI Divisions of the regular army being formed. The remainder of the unit were formed into the 1st, 2nd and 3rd Regiments and the 4th Cavalry Regiment. (*Vitetti Archive*)

(**Opposite, below**) Benito Mussolini in the last months of his life inspects a unit of the Brigate Nere, the Brigate Nere Mobile Alpina at Salo in March 1945. The Italian dictator still had the loyalty of some of the Italian population in what was a deeply divided country. Small well-armed units like this were capable of dealing with partisans but were not really trained to fight the mechanised formations of the Allies advancing through the country. When this photograph was taken Mussolini had less than two months to live; he was shot by partisans on 29 April. (*Author's Collection, Public Domain*)

Paolo Bragadin of the Garibaldi Chichero Division receives Allied supplies dropped over the Aveto Valley. The brigades of the Chichero Division based in Liguria played an important role in the liberation of Genoa. An insurrection took place on the night of 23 April 1945 and lasted until the 26th, with Allied troops arriving the next day. His men have gathered the air-dropped supplies to be sorted out and then sent to the various units of the division. (*Author's Collection, Public Domain*)

Pompea Calajani, known as 'Barbato', is seen standing on parade in an Italian town. He was one of the most influential leaders of the Garibaldi formations. Born in 1906 he was a staunch anti-Fascist from his 20s and was arrested for his activities against the Mussolini regime. He was called up in 1940 to serve in the army as a cavalryman but constantly plotted within its ranks against the Fascists. In 1943 he joined a local partisan band quickly rising through the ranks of the Garibaldi, becoming commander of the 4th Brigade in Cuneo. 'Barbato' organised the April 1945 march on Turin, which had taken the city by 28 April. During the liberation of the city his men cooperated with opposition 'Justice & Freedom' partisans in defeating a strong force of Brigate Nere fighters. (*Author's Collection, Public Domain*)

Women partisans pose proudly with their submachine guns in a liberated city in Northern Italy in 1945. Female volunteers didn't fight in numbers with the partisans but they joined groups like the 'Groups of Patriotic Resistance' (GAP), 'Women's Defence Groups', and others. They helped in every aspect of the partisan war and often suffered the same consequences as their male comrades if caught by the Germans and Fascist Italians. These three women are armed with a pair of Beretta MB-38s and a US M2 'grease gun' submachine gun. (*Author's Collection, Public Domain*)

(**Above**) A column of the 'Gabriele Camozzi' partisan Brigade of the Giustizia e Liberta formations of the Action Party march through the town they have liberated. Brigades of the second largest partisan group sometimes cooperated with the larger Garibaldini formations. This group operated in the Seriana Valley from May 1944 until the end of the fighting in Italy. G & L units were known for their professionalism and for the high casualty rate among their officers and leaders, with 4,500 killed during the fighting. (*Author's Collection, Public Domain*)

(**Opposite, above**) A group of Italian partisans are seen in St Marks Square in the centre of Venice after the city's liberation on 27 April 1945. Like other Northern Italian cities, the local partisan network waited until the time was right to plan Venice's liberation. Political prisoners who had been held in the city's Santa Maria Maggiore prison were released to join in the liberation. Fighting with German defenders continued into the 28th with battles taking place in the Piazzale Roma and around the harbour, and the final surrender took place on the 29th. (*Author's Collection, Public Domain*)

(**Opposite, below**) In February 1945 a unit of partisans attended a ceremony at which their commander was awarded an Italian bravery medal. They belong to the 28th 'Mario Gordini' Garibaldi Brigade, which was commanded by the Communist politician Arrigo Boldrini. Like other well organised partisan brigades the fighters of the 28th have been issued with some British military uniforms which they are wearing with civilian items. The tricolour rosettes on their army issue berets were a feature of partisan uniforms and they are armed with Lee Enfield No.4 rifles and a Sten Mark 2 submachine gun. (*Author's Collection, Public Domain*)

During a victory parade two men of the Ossola Valley partisans carry their comrade to his seat. The Ossola partisans wore their own unique uniform made from brown woollen cloth with red collar tabs with edelweiss badges attached. These partisans operated on the Swiss-Italian border and must have had workshops to produce these uniforms. Standard headgear was a brown woollen Alpini hat, usually with a crow's feather as worn by the Italian Alpini to this day. (*Author's Collection, Public Domain*)

(**Above**) Garibaldi partisans march through a town in North-Western Italy having liberated it from the German garrison. They carry the flag of the Garibaldini, with the Italian tricolour having a red star edged in yellow with a white circle in the centre and a green inner circle. It was the usual practice for any partisan group taking a town or city, either with or without Allied assistance, to set up a committee as their first attempt at administrating the population. (*Author's Collection, Public Domain*)

(**Right**) Partisans of the 'Chichero' Garibaldi Division walk through the newly liberated city of Genoa in Liguria following the surrender of the German garrison. The city was liberated after the victory of an insurrection which lasted from 23 April 1945 until the evening of the 26th. Troops of the US 5th Army marched into the city on the 27th after the partisans had seized the port, which was the largest in Italy. (*Author's Collection, Public Domain*)

Chapter Ten

French Resistance 1940-1944

Resistance to German and Italian occupation in France began in the same way that it did in other occupied European countries like Belgium, the Netherlands, Denmark and Norway from 1940. Small groups of resisters emerged almost immediately, often formed around a group of friends or a family unit who took part in relatively minor acts of sabotage. They published underground newspapers and sent intelligence to the British and set up an escape network for airman shot down behind German lines. Disparate French resistance groups were united in November 1942 into the 'National Resistance Council'. For several years the resistance usually known as the Maquis concentrated their efforts in the southern part of France under the rule of Marshal Petain's Vichy government. In January 1943 the Maquis infiltrated the German Occupied Zone for the first time, and on the 26th the three main movements of the Southern Zone were amalgamated into the Mouvements unis de la Résistance (MUR). This group largely followed their leader Paul Moulin's policy of building up strength ready for a future showdown with the Vichy and Germans.

In contrast, the Francs-Tireurs et Partisans (FTP) wanted to act as soon as possible against their enemies. In April 1942 the FTP had effectively been formed as the Communist resistance group. They accepted members who were not Communists but the leadership was totally controlled by the left-wingers. In June 1943 the French resistance was left rudderless by the arrest and death of their inspirational leader Paul Moulin. It became apparent that they had relied too much on a single man who was constantly under threat of arrest. His direct contact and close relationship with the French in London was lost, leaving the resistance leadership bereft.

The resistance did survive Moulin's loss and by the summer of 1943 there were an estimated 13,000 resisters throughout France, largely comprising young working-class youths under the age of 25. By early 1944 the FTP had a strength of 100,000 fighters and in March these were placed officially under the authority of the Forces Francaises de L'interieur by General de Gaulle. De Gaulle announced in October 1944 that the FFI was now be part of the Free French Army and that its command structure should be better organised. From now on a unit of thirty men would be commanded by a sous-lieutenant, 100 men by a lieutenant and 300 men by a capitaine. Larger units of 1,000 men would be commanded by a commandant and 2,000 men by a lieutenant-colonel. On 12 June 1944 German Field-Marshal Von Rundstedt said that FFI fighters would never be recognised as regular fighters. He went on to say that any resister captured, whether man or woman or youth, should be immediately executed.

From June 1944 the estimated 200,000 strong 'French Forces of the Interior' (FFI) were linked to the Allied 'Supreme Headquarters Allied Expeditionary Force' (SHAEF).

They were put under the command of General Marie Pierre Koening on 23 June whose role was to unify all French resistance forces. This allowed the FFI to become a vital part of the 'Overlord' (Invasion of Normandy) and 'Anvil' (Invasion of Southern France – Provence). Allied plans were for the FFI to seize bridges and prepare the towns and cities of France for the Allied advances. According to US General Patton the advance of his forces would not have been possible without the aid of the FFI.

French resistance in the Vichy controlled Southern Zone was led by the Armée Secrète, which was a collective of three Gaullist resistance movements. This disparate group of French resistance organisations was made up of Liberation-Sud, Francs-Tireurs and Combat. In the summer of 1942 the Commander-in-Chief of the Armée Secrète, General Delestraint, had secretly toured the Southern French countryside. He was looking for regions which included mountainous terrain that could be occupied by resistance groups and established as natural strongholds. His plan was that when the time was right these 'bastions' could be established as centres of resistance within Vichy- and German-held territory. During his tour he noted several places where armed groups could hold out and provide an obstacle to the German defence of France when the expected Allied invasion began. In the Haute Savoie Department in South-Eastern France in January 1944, the Plateau des Glières was being used as a dropping zone by Allied planes to drop arms to the local Maquis. The Maquis were determined to hold on to this strategic base and fought a bitter struggle for two months and involving 467 resisters. They were faced by superior Milice forces but held out until 26 March, when they made an orderly withdrawal having lost 129 fighters.

In the Haute Loire Department of South-Eastern France a 1,200 strong Maquis force held another rocky redoubt, close to the town of Le Puy-en-Velay in the summer of 1944. The defenders were well armed and many had been issued with uniforms and were organised into six companies, the 31st to 36th. The armed Maquis fighters were supported by another 400 unarmed men and youths who helped them to besiege the German-held town with its 600- to 700-strong garrison. When the Germans tried to break out of the town in mid-August 1944, 500 were captured by the Maquis while another 150 were killed in their trucks as they tried to escape down the mountain roads. Also in South-Eastern France was the Vercors plateau which was thirty miles long and fifteen miles wide and was near to the town of Grenoble. It was held in June 1944 by 3,000 Maquis which included fifty former Colonial troops who had been forced to do hard labour by the Germans. The Maquis used this stronghold to launch raids on the Milice and German garrisons and they had to act to crush their defiance. When the Milice and Germans attacked they were faced by well armed Maquis who held out until September.

The Maquis' lack of heavy weaponry meant that their only option was to withdraw into the countryside surrounding the plateau. They withdrew along mountain paths and managed to get most of their fighters past the surrounding Milice and Germans, losing only 100 men in the battle. On 10 June 1944 the FFI commander Koenig had ordered the resistance not to engage in costly 'Insurrection Nationale', the name given to the costly insurrections that took place at Gileres Plateau and on Mount Mouchat. Instead he insisted that small groups of the FFI should keep their attacks small scale so as not to provoke reprisals by the Germans and Milice.

This announcement had been made four days after the Allied landings in Normandy on 6 June 1944, which would change the whole trajectory of the French resistance. 'Operation Dragoon', the landing of Allied forces in the South of France on 15 August, saw thousands of FFI fighters aiding the Allied advances in Northern and Southern France. In Southern France 75,000 fighters were cooperating with the Allies, which included large numbers of Free French troops. The relationship between the hard-fighting Free French troops and the less disciplined FFI fighters was not always good. Small arms were liberally handed out to the FFI by the Allies but their lack of training and battle experience was noted by the regulars. During late 1944 and early 1945 some FFI were organised into regular units, such as the 49th Infantry Regiment and the 3rd Demi-Brigade of Chasseurs. By the end of the war FFI personnel had been organised into sixty-eight infantry regiments, two special forces battalions, twenty light infantry battalions, one tank battalion, sixteen artillery regiments, two AA regiments, five engineer regiments and three construction regiments.

In total, 500,000 French people were actively involved in the resistance, but this was far from a mass movement. Many French men and women chose to neither resist or collaborate, and in fact the resistance was made up of less than 2 per cent of the French population. Those that did resist paid a heavy price with about 100,000, or one in five, of the resistance dying in action, being executed, or sent to concentration camps. At the end of the fighting in France collaborators were also to pay a heavy price with 9,000 Milice para-military police and members of Vichy political organisations being shot. Up to 30,000 mostly young French women, usually described as 'horizontal collaborators', were punished by having their heads shaven in public. Their crime was to form genuine relationships with German soldiers, or sleeping with the occupiers in return for scarce rations or silk stockings.

The French resistance fighters often arrived at their forest and mountain bases wearing basic civilian clothing which wore out quickly when worn every day in the field. It was a case of make do and mend for the fighters unless they were lucky to have a unit seamstress or tailor. One of these young men is repairing the seat of his comrade's pants while he is at his station on guard duty. (*Author's Collection, Public Domain*)

(**Above**) Three fighters of the Corsican Maquis undergo training with their recently delivered Sten Mk III submachine guns. The resistance on the island was initially scattered and limited in its objectives, especially after the huge influx of Italian occupiers. By 1943 they had learned much about the enemy and did not fear the Italians as much as they earlier had. They were better organised and had established contact with the Allies and began to receive arms in some numbers. (*Author's Collection, Public Domain*)

(**Opposite, above**) This Corsican Maquis is part of an ambush waiting for an Italian unit which has ventured into their territory. The rugged mountainous terrain was a great advantage to the Corsicans, with 90 per cent of the island covered in this rough country. It was reported that the Maquis on Corsica totalled 3,000 and controlled 115 villages, but these fighters were not affiliated with the FFI. They fought under the banner of the Fronte Nationale and rejected attempts by the main French resistance to bring them under their wing. (*Author's Collection, Public Domain*)

(**Opposite, below**) A well armed Corsican Maquis unit of seven fighters poses with their armoury of Sten Mk III submachine guns at Sainte-Marie Sicche on 13 September 1943. Only one young man, presumably the junior member of the group, has a French Army revolver. During 1943 a total of six Allied submarines secretly visited the island bringing new fighters and small arms, which boosted morale. By 8 September it was reported that the Corsican resistance had a total of 10,000 Sten guns. (*Author's Collection, Public Domain*)

(**Above**) Italian soldiers making up the occupation force of Corsica wait at the docks of one of the ports of the island after disembarking. The Italian VII Corps was made up of the 20th 'Friuli Infantry Division, the 44th 'Cremona' Infantry Division and two poorly trained coastal divisions, the 225th and 226th. There was also a battalion of Alpini mountain troops and an armoured battalion, and from March 1943 a Corsican Labour Battalion. At first some Corsicans were supportive of the Italians but the majority did not want any kind of occupation, no matter how light handed. (*Author's Collection, Public Domain*)

(**Opposite, above**) An Italian Army Semovente 47mm self-propelled gun stands guard over the port of Bastica in Corsica in early 1943. When the Italians took over the island in November 1942 they arrived in large numbers, but by the spring of 1943 they were losing control. The Corsican Maquis were far too weak to threaten the Italian and German control of the ports and cities of the island. They were, however, able to maintain a strong presence in the poorly populated interior of the island. (*Author's Collection, Public Domain*)

(**Opposite, below**) This Corsican Maquisard is operating a radio supplied by the Allies to pass on any relevant intelligence. It was important to constantly move any radio equipment around to stop the German and Italian occupiers discovering its location. Skilled radio operators were at a premium in war-time France, and capturing or killing them was as important as destroying their equipment. (*Author's Collection, Public Domain*)

Young men of the Maquis take shelter while they get their lunch in the cover of the undergrowth. Many of these young men had joined the resistance groups to avoid conscription and they had to prove their motives to the local population. The main rule for surviving as a resistance fighter before June 1944 was not to stay in the same place for too long. (*Author's Collection, Public Domain*)

Armed with a captured Mauser 98k rifle, an older fighter of the Maquis looks out for any signs of the enemy from a tree. The resistance was largely based in the South of France where there was more suitable terrain to build any encampments. Maquis came from the word for the scrubland which grew in Southern France and was also described as 'thicket' or 'bush'. This name was also used to describe the armed groups which operated before the Allied invasion of Normandy in June 1944. (*Author's Collection, Public Domain*)

The young FFI fighter in the foreground of this photograph is wearing what appears to be a jacket from one of the Vichy-organised youth movements and he has an Adrian steel helmet. It was probably taken from one of the enemy, as few if any former Vichy supporters were accepted into the ranks of the FFI. Resistance policy towards Vichy collaborators was 'no amnesty, no pardon, no quarter'. (*Author's Collection, Public Domain*)

Maquisards clean their small armoury of weapons in their forest base with one man having a German Maxim M08/15 machine gun. Although not totally clear, it appears that one man has a Sten MkII and another has some kind of rifle and an automatic pistol. The resistance made complaints about the lack of weapons, but during 1944 the supply of Allied arms increased drastically. (*Author's Collection, Public Domain*)

(**Above**) Two FFI fighters share some intelligence with their US Army colleagues in the first weeks after the Normandy landings. Of course the French were keen to help the British and US military as much as possible, but the relationship was not always cordial. Some resistance leaders were Communists and resented the presence of foreign forces on their soil even though they were Allies. Others may have been resentful that their proud nation was relying on foreign powers to liberate them from Nazi rule. (*Author's Collection, Public Domain*)

(**Opposite, above**) Three young Maquis bask in the sun showing off their weaponry to a local photographer in the South of France. The weaponry suggests that they have had direct contact with the Allied forces as Lee Enfield .303 rifles were not air dropped to the resistance. Their prized possession would be the MG-42 machine gun held by the man stood up while the man in the centre has a Sten MKII submachine gun. (*Author's Collection, Public Domain*)

(**Opposite, below**) A line of FFI fighters in 1944 show the variety of paramilitary dress mixed with civilian and military clothing worn by the men. Some have FFI armbands on and one man has acquired a black painted Adrian helmet from the Vichy police. One of the men is armed with a Berthier rifle, while others have German Mausers and the man second from the right has a US M2 carbine. (*Author's Collection, Public Domain*)

An FFI instructor shows his comrades what arms have been air dropped into the Haute Loire region by the RAF. Of course the resistance fighters needed to familiarise themselves with this new weaponry before using it on an operation. While the instructor holds a Sten MkII, the pistols piled on the table include a Colt revolver and automatic pistols, as well as Ruby and Le Francois pistols and a Bulldog revolver. (*Author's Collection, Public Domain*)

A Maquis sentry uses a wall for cover as he looks for enemy movements against the Haute Loire defences. The defenders of the Haute Loire had acquired a large number of small arms, including British Sten MkII guns like this man, and a few ex-French Army MAS-36 rifles. He is wearing an Adrian helmet which may have been brought back to his home by a demobilised relative in 1940. (*Author's Collection, Public Domain*)

A group of FFI fighters examine some of the weapons that have been dropped to them by the RAF in the early months of 1944. During late 1943 the FFI in the six regions of Southern France complained about the lack of weaponry supplied to them. They had tried to find their own arms from hidden caches left from the days of the defeat during the French Campaign in 1940. Region three fighters had only a few dozen mixed rifles and forty machine guns which had been retrieved from a lake! Region two FFI units had total of 151 rifles, seven heavy and two light machine guns and five boxes of grenades to arm several thousand fighters. (*Author's Collection, Public Domain*)

A young Maquisard poses with his US supplied M1 carbine, one of the most popular weapons supplied by the Allies. In June 1944 in the immediate aftermath of D-Day 5,505 of the carbines were delivered to the French resistance along with 2 million rounds of ammunition. The grenades tucked into his belt are a mixture of a German stick type and what appears to be a Russian model. This man is in fact a Ukrainian who was part of a work construction and work battalion in the German Army. Having escaped from his unit he was captured by the French resistance who gave him a chance to fight with them against the Germans. (US National Archives)

A Maquis court interrogates a woman who may be suspected of giving information to the German or Vichy authorities. The resistance's fear of informers was well founded with whole groups of the resistance being betrayed by a few careless words. Often threats would be made to potential informers by the Germans or their French Milice forces. French collaborators were hated by the Maquis and assassinations of Vichy officials was one of their main tactics. (*Author's Collection, Public Domain*)

US Army soldiers hand out weapons to a unit of the FFI which appears to include two Black soldiers. Although the Frenchmen appear to be asking about the weapons they had been given, the Lee Enfield rifle and the Sten MKII submachine guns would be unfamiliar to the Americans. The man on the right, however, is armed with a US M2 carbine which would of course be well known to the Americans. (*Author's Collection, Public Domain*)

During the street fighting to liberate a French town an FFI fighter uses the cover of a military truck to fire his Sten Mk II gun. As the Allied armies advanced into France after D-Day, groups of FFI tried to assist them by starting uprisings behind German lines. This was a tricky business as the Germans, although slowly withdrawing from Normandy in Central France, were still capable of brutally crushing any resistance activities. (*Author's Collection, Public Domain*)

This FFI fighter is posing in front of the German military signs outside of the city of Rennes. These signs would be torn down but the cameraman has decided to take this man's picture for posterity. Rennes in Brittany was liberated on 4 August by a force made up of FFI and the US 8th Infantry Division led by General George S. Patton. The Frenchman has been issued with a US steel helmet, a Mauser 98k rifle and has an armband on his sleeve which says he is a temporary policeman. (*Author's Collection, Public Domain*)

FFI men line the streets of a French town to welcome Allied troops with an expectant crowd behind them. When German forces withdrew from a village, town or city it was the role of the FFI to hassle them. On a number of occasions the FFI took control of cities and towns, sometimes meeting little resistance from the demoralised German garrisons. On other occasions they faced fanatical SS and other units who wanted to fight to the last man, causing heavy casualties for the French. (*Author's Collection, Public Domain*)

A group of mixed US soldiers and FFI volunteers sort out what arms and equipment are available for the Frenchmen. One FFI man is trying to familiarise himself with a P-17 rifle, while the man in the vest is also holding the same type of rifle. Arms seem to have been handed out to anyone who could convince the Allies that they were willing to use them to attack the nearest German or Vichy force. (*Author's Collection, Public Domain*)

A proud Maquisard stands outside a café with a Bren gun, which is being admired by the crowd around him. For some members of the resistance the esteem of being involved in the overthrow of the German occupation made them heroes for the rest of their lives. On the other side, having been involved with the Vichy government in any context could mark a person for life. This is, of course, if they were fortunate to survive the immediate aftermath of the German occupation. (*Author's Collection, Public Domain*)

(**Above**) A Maquisard armed with a Sten MkII submachine gun in Marseille is preparing to move forward with the support of US Army officer Lieutenant Edwin E. Dowell. The photograph was taken between 21 and 28 August as street battles took place in the important Southern French port. (*Author's Collection, Public Domain*)

(**Opposite, above**) Enthusiastic Maquisards gather around a US Army instructor in the summer of 1944 to learn about the workings of a captured German MG-34 general purpose machine gun. Thousands of ordinary young French men and women were issued with rifles, submachine guns and machine guns in 1944. Carrying a firearm gave these young people a status that they could never have hoped to experience, even if it only lasted for a few weeks or months in 1944. (NARA)

(**Opposite, below**) Men of the Milice are on parade armed with captured Lee Enfield rifles and wearing the distinctive beret with their insignia on it. The Greek letter 'Gamma' was chosen as the symbol of the Milice as representing the 'charging and headstrong ram'. On 24 April 1943 the Milice suffered their first casualty at the hands of the resistance, which was to be the first of many during the struggle between these pro-Vichy forces and their bitter enemies. (*Author's Collection, Public Domain*)

Milice men bring in a group of French resisters for interrogation and mostly likely execution, as they battled their FFI foes in July 1944. The resistance feared the Milice more than they did the Gestapo or even the SS because their fellow Frenchmen knew their habits, their ways and their dialects. With up to 30,000 men in the Milice they became a real threat to the existence of the FFI and were more hated than the Germans. (*Author's Collection, Public Domain*)

Miliciens march past their commander in 1944 armed with weaponry taken from the British Expeditionary Forces in June 1940. They were armed with French rifles and machine guns but many photographs show them using Sten guns and other weaponry captured from arms drops sent to the resistance. (*Author's Collection, Public Domain*)

This Milice guard outside a Vichy government building is wearing a black painted M1926 steel helmet with his dark blue tunic and trousers. He is armed with the MAS-36 rifle which the standard type in service with the French Army in 1940. Those who joined the Milice were either right-wingers, men with a grudge against the Allies, and criminals offered pardons. Also all Milice personnel were safe from deportation as forced labour to Germany, as were their families. (*Author's Collection, Public Domain*)

A line of young women fighters of the FFI pose in their military uniforms with several having grenades on their belts. Women, especially young women, paid an important part in the FFI but their presence was not always welcome. Some officers thought that their male comrades would be too protective of the fairer sex in action and that this would affect their fighting abilities. (*Author's Collection, Public Domain*)

This female Maquisard became famous in the Western press, toting her prized MP-40 submachine gun during the liberation of Chartres in September 1944. Simone Seguin was just one of many young women who took up arms during the summer of 1944 but her photograph seems to have been featured more than others. (*NARA*)

Women made up an important part of the French resistance with up to 20 per cent of its members being females. Although they did take part in fighting their role tended to be more intelligence and other non-combat roles. This did not protect them from any retaliations by the German and Vichy security forces and 15 per cent of all deportations to concentration camps were female. This young woman is pictured probably in her home village with a captured Mauser 98k rifle over her shoulder. Allied news cameramen saw an attractive woman with a rifle as an image the people of the US and the world would be interested in seeing. (*Author's Collection, Public Domain*)

An older FFI fighter reads one of the resistance newspapers to his young female comrade who is armed with a US Thompson submachine gun. She also had a rifle of some type over her left shoulder which she will presumably hand over to a fighter who is unarmed. The leaders of FFI units would attach anything appropriate to their clothes to show their status within the resistance group. This man will have an FFI armband on his left arm and could also have a cloth or metal badge which shows his allegiance to the Forces Francaises de l'Intérieur. (*Author's Collection, Public Domain*)

Once the German army had left a town or village, then the built up anger was taken out on anyone accused of collaborating with the occupiers. Girls and women who had 'fraternised' with the Germans were lucky to escape with the shaving or rough cutting off of their hair. This FFI official holds on to a local girl while his comrade hacks at her hair after which she would be humiliated in front of her neighbours and townsfolk. (*Author's Collection, Public Domain*)

(**Above**) Laughing FFI fighters drag young women away from the building where they had had their hair publicly shorn off. Those females who had betrayed secrets to the enemy could expect worse treatment, but these girls will have to live out their lives among the people who had humiliated them. Most women and girls had slept with German soldiers or given them sexual favours in turn for rations or other treats, but some had had genuine love affairs with the enemy. (*Author's Collection, Public Domain*)

(**Opposite, above**) This poorly armed unit of FFI fighters illustrates the shortage of weaponry among the resistance before the Allied invasion. Although not all the group are visible several of the men have their arms behind their backs as if to show they are not armed. It was calculated in 1943 that every six-man unit should have two submachine guns, two automatic pistols and twelve grenades. At least 300 rounds of ammunition for the submachine guns would be needed, while the pistols needed an initial twenty-five rounds. Calculating the monthly average of ammunition use a further ten rounds for the submachine guns and five for the pistols would be required to keep the six men in the field. (*Author's Collection, Public Domain*)

Two brothers chat before going on a mission with their FFI unit, with one brother having a German MG-34 machine gun over his shoulder. His brother carries spare ammunition belts for the machine gun and is armed only with a German stick grenade. Although the MG-34 had a great rate of firing, with 900 round per minute, this created a problem. Most FFI units had to very sparing with its use as they would be lucky to more than a handful of fifty or 250 round belts of ammunition making extended firing a rare event. (*Author's Collection*, *Public Domain*)

(**Above**) Resistance fighters who are unarmed are helping the Allied advance as best they can by removing a burning vehicle from the path of a column of Sherman tanks. When arms were handed out to the Maquis by the Allies there was little distinction made between veteran fighters and new volunteers. The situation was chaotic and small arms could be claimed by anyone who said they were willing to fight the Germans. (*Author's Collection, Public Domain*)

(**Opposite, above**) The coffin of an FFI fighter is carried to his home for burial after he was killed in the Eastern-Pyrenees in 1943. Losses of the FFI were reported to total over 90,000, with most shot in action or in revenge while others were tortured or deported by the German and Vichy authorities. Both sides killed civil servants and officials, with Vichy officials being constantly targeted by the resistance. When captured in the field FFI fighters were usually shot immediately unless the occupiers thought they may have vital intelligence. (*Author's Collection, Public Domain*)

(**Opposite, below**) Young Maquisards take part in training in their base in the Vercors region in preparation for defending it against German and Vichy forces. The Vercors plateau, close to the city of Grenoble in South-Eastern France, was partly mountainous and partly forested. At 50km deep and 25km across and surrounded by four rivers, it appeared to be a natural bastion which looked like it could be easily defended. This perceived impregnable fortress was to prove not as easy to defend as it seemed when the Milice and Germans attacked in force in January 1944. (*Author's Collection, Public Domain*)

Jacques Chaban-Delmas held the rank of brigade-general in the Free French forces and acted as General De Gaulle's liaison between him and the FFI in Paris. The 29-year-old warned de Gaulle that he believed the French Communist resistance wanted to kill up to '150,000 for nothing'. As in other occupied countries in Europe, the Communist and other resistance groups in France were at odds with each other throughout the war. (*Author's Collection, Public Domain*)

The first signs of resistance by the Parisian FFI was the building of barricades and sandbagged positions on street corners on 19 August 1944. This hastily built sandbag barricade is manned by a woman and man who have acquired steel helmets, one French and one German, but have few arms. They are facing the German garrison of Paris which numbered up to 30,000 troops, including 3,000 fanatical SS. The garrison also had eighty tanks, including the potent Panther and Tiger tanks from the 9th Panzer Division. German artillery in Paris was made up of twenty-three field guns, thirty-five anti-tank guns and six smaller guns of various types. (*Author's Collection, Public Domain*)

This sandbagged position in the centre of Paris is defended by a motley group of poorly armed FFI fighters. From this poor quality photograph it appears that their armoury is made up of a French light machine gun, a carbine, and what might be a sporting rifle. They do have a few automatic pistols but it was going to hard for the FFI to follow the leaders' instructions that every man from 18 to 50 should be armed. General De Gaulle was determined that Paris should not become another Warsaw, with its buildings destroyed when its poorly armed defenders could no longer resist. (*Author's Collection, Public Domain*)

FFI fighters fire towards German-held positions from a hotel window during the early days of the liberation of Paris. Few Germans came onto the streets during the liberation, preferring to stay in their strongholds throughout the city. This group is fairly typical of the small units of the FFI before the arrival of the French 2nd Armoured Division on 24 August. They appear to have a single French Lebel carbine and a few clips to reload it with, as well as a few hand grenades. (*Author's Collection, Public Domain*)

(**Above**) A Bren machine gun is fired from an apartment window in the final days of the liberation of Paris by FFI fighters. Although the men have acquired a British Bren gun with a few spare clips, they have only a single automatic pistol with which to give the crew cover. The main weapon available to the resistance in Paris was the Molotov cocktail, which the FFI threw at passing German vehicles. When the Germans did sally out in their heavy and medium tanks they caused havoc and it proved difficult to disable them with hopefully thrown petrol bombs. (*Author's Collection, Public Domain*)

(**Opposite, above**) German officers, at great risk to themselves, speak through the iron grill of a window on the Chamber of Deputies building in Paris to negotiate with the FFI gathering outside. There were 400 German troops holding out in the building and their spokesman will no doubt be getting abuse from the FFI fighters with their tricolour flag. These kind of negotiations took place throughout Paris as the Germans hoped to be allowed to surrender to the Allied forces arriving in the city. (*Author's Collection*)

(**Opposite, below**) These jubilant FFI fighters have captured an SS officer in the city of Chartres, south-west of Paris. During the fighting for Paris it was often diehard SS units, or even individuals, who continued to fire on the crowds, killing a number of Parisians. However, many of the dead were reported to have been killed by 'friendly fire' from young trigger-happy FFI fighters unused to the weaponry they had been given without any training. Many captured SS men were dealt with out of sight, in revenge for the numerous atrocities they had inflicted on the French people. (*Author's Collection*)

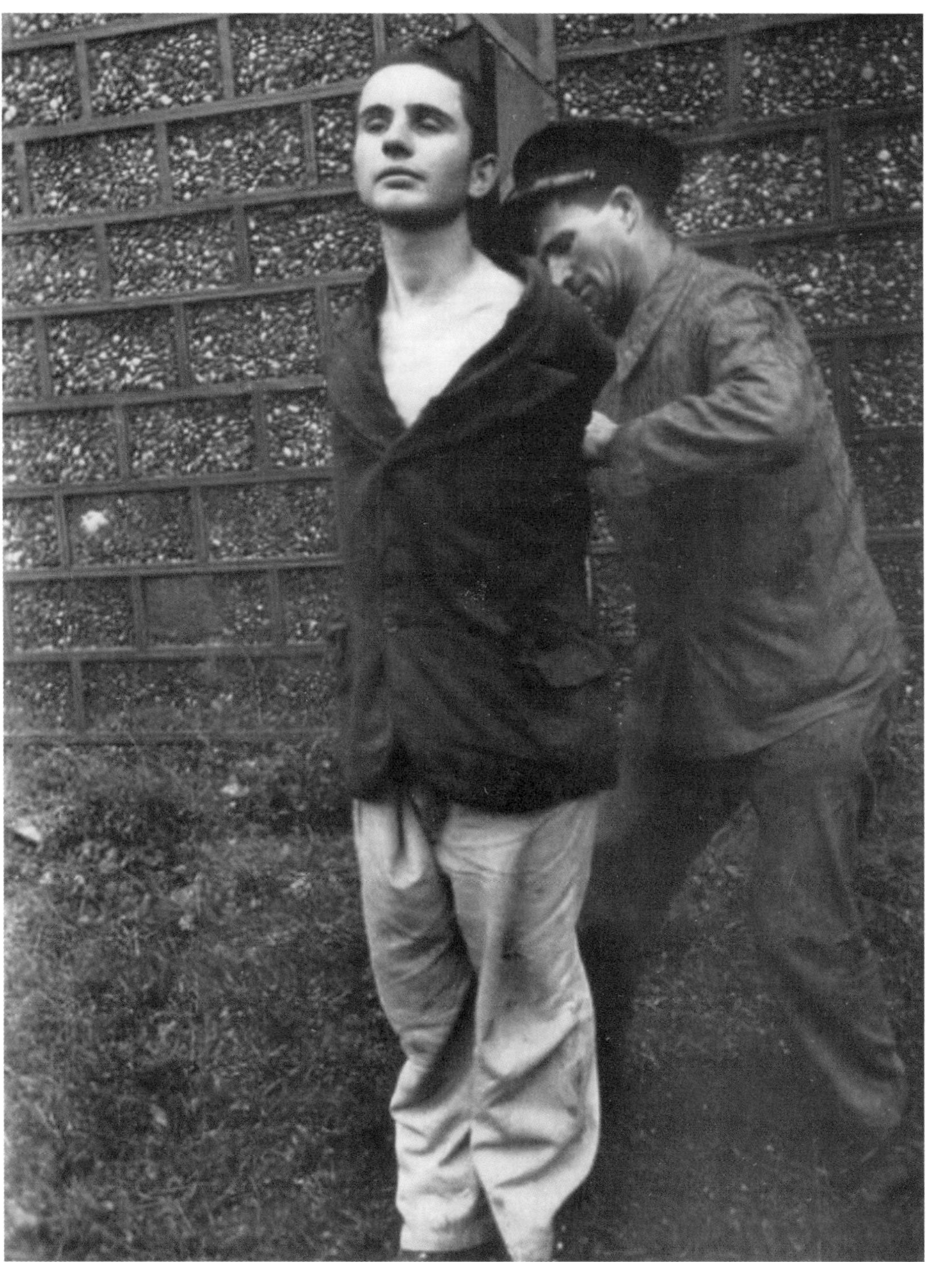

A member of the Vichy Chantiers de Jeunesse Francaise youth movement is tied to a post before being executed by firing squad at the end of the war in France. Formed in 1940, the youth movement was supposed to be compulsory for all French youths in unoccupied France. In 1944 the CJF was disbanded, but hardcore Vichy supporters continued to serve the puppet regime. This young man has been found guilty of going beyond the usual collaboration of some youths in Vichy France. Age and sex was no protection for anyone who had collaborated with the Germans, and many like this youth were swiftly dealt with when they fell into resistance hands. (*Author's Collection*)